"Other than that, I have no opinion"

CHUCK SNYDER

Tyndale House
Publishers, Inc.
Wheaton, Illinois

To my sweet wife, Barb,
   whose love enriches me daily.
To a perfect son, Tim,
   and to a perfect daughter, Bev.

All Scripture is from *The Living Bible,* copyright
1971 by Tyndale House Publishers, Inc.,
Wheaton, Illinois.

The author's royalties are being donated to
Living Bibles International.

First printing, May 1985
Library of Congress Catalog Card Number 85–50028
ISBN 0-8423-4763-1

CONTENTS

INTRODUCTION

I suppose everyone at one time or another has had a dream about writing a book. The strongest and most elementary reason is probably a desire to share something that is near to our hearts with the people we know.

I have the feeling that many churches teach us how to look, talk, and act like Christians on Sunday, but the teaching seems to have no particular relevance to the rest of the week. This book is intended to show what life can be all during the week, walking down paths strewn with boulders and hard spots. And when we fall through anger, bitterness, or a thousand other human failings, I want others to see that there is a way for us to get up, dust ourselves off, and get back on the path again.

We cannot live the kind of life we should on our own, no matter how hard we try. I'm a "Type A" personality—an independent spirit. I used to get terribly depressed when things didn't go my way. I tend to be an angry person—resentful—with bitterness welling up in me from time to time. I'm impatient. I have been known to reject people when they'd get in my way or didn't do things on my timetable. I guess you could say that I am often a walking example of what God does NOT want us to be. But since the bottom line of Christianity is God's unconditional love, I know he hasn't given up on me yet. He is turning me around in so many areas of my life!

It's a slow process. I'm still on the "easel," and expect to be there the rest of my life, being painted into the picture God wants me to be. In the process, I'm learning how to love as God wants me to love. He is giving me insights into why I should act and love differently than what my natural inclination suggests. Because of God's continuing work in me, I feel that he has given me some of these experiences to share with you. And maybe you can learn from my failures. My goal is to let other people, who have the same struggles I do, know that there is hope for us, not just on Sunday as we do our Christian "thing," but on Monday when we meet the boss, try to talk to our kids, communicate with our parents, husbands or wives, when we get cut off on the freeway, or try to love the unlovely. God is not just some big unreachable, untouchable, unreal force. He is a living Person, who wants to influence every waking moment and to give meaning and purpose to our lives.

I ask you not to put off reading this book because you think it will have a whole bunch of religious jargon and phrases that you won't understand. I've tried to eliminate all that stuff. Just breeze on through those things you don't understand. This is not intended to be a "religious" book. Religion often sounds stuffy and pious and self-righteous, and I don't want you to think of me that way. I hope you'll laugh, maybe cry with me, as I tell my story. Most of all, I hope you'll enjoy it, whether you agree with what I've come to believe or not.

I want to warn you, though.

The book may be hazardous to some of your long-standing beliefs, opinions, feelings, doctrines, prejudices, leanings, dogmas, evaluations, impressions, estimations, or hunches.

Please read all of it before rejecting, hanging, drawing and quartering, tar and feathering, rebuffing, or drowning the author!

ONE

66 I Was Born at a Very Early Age 99

I was born in Seattle, Washington, raised in Tacoma, and spent some time on a farm near Coulee City, Washington. I settled my family in Seattle and will probably be here the rest of my life. How's that for a quick biography?

I had an extremely happy home life. Some of my most delightful memories were the times my mom and I played horseshoes or some indoor games with the family in the evening. I can't remember anything negative about my home or the way I was treated by my parents.

However, I did have problems with self-confidence in my earlier years. I remember so well walking down the streets of my hometown, sure that everyone was looking and laughing at me. When I saw a group of kids over in the corner at school, I was sure I was the target of ridicule. In hindsight, I guess I *wasn't* their target, because several times I was elected president of this, chairman of that, student body president, and president of the young people's group. It proves again, I suppose, that a person does not have to be unloved and misunderstood to feel uneasy and lacking in self-confidence.

Although my parents insisted I go to church, God had very little to do with my life and the Bible was a blank book to me. When I went away to college, I had a passing conversation with God once in a while when I got into trouble, but nothing too meaningful. While in college, I went to church occasionally out of guilt, I suppose, then wouldn't go again for some time since church really didn't mean much to me. Most of the pastors and teachers in my life had given me the impression that they had perfect marriages, perfect children, perfect thought lives, spent two hours reading the Bible every day, three hours in prayer, and that they would be shocked to think a Christian would ever have the kind of problems I had. When I had a struggle, the last person in the world I would think about going to for help was the pastor or Sunday school teacher. They just wouldn't be able to understand a Christian having problems, I thought.

I couldn't relate to many of the kids in church either. I felt inferior at school since my "Christianity" kept me from participating in many of the school social activities, and low self-esteem kept me out of sports. One of my physical education instructors in high school put us through some running drills, and he said that I would make a terrific football player—loose hips or something like that. He thought I should turn out, so one day I brought my new unused jeans to school and was going to try to make the team. However, on the way to the field, one of the older kids who was already on the squad said something like, "You are going to turn out for football?"

I mumbled something, and after he left, I headed home instead of the football field—an NFL superstar nipped in the bud because of low self-esteem.

My last day of high school I played my guitar and sang in a talent contest. I got a standing ovation, and kids came up to me afterward, amazed that I could do anything like that, wondering why I had waited so long to perform. I just said, "Thanks," and looked back on what might have been, had I felt a little more confidence in myself.

I went to college to become a veterinarian because I love kids and animals. I'm forever escorting spiders outside who get trapped in the sink, or tipping beetles right side up, or fishing bumble bees out of the swimming pool.

Even though I loved animals while I was growing up, I was a loner when it came to people. College was a little threatening because I didn't know anyone and really didn't know how to meet or talk to strangers. We ate with the girls at the school cafeteria in college. I liked girls a whole lot better than boys, and had a lot of girl "friends," but none of the smoochy kind. I worshiped from afar, without the courage to make any real advances.

One day I noticed a note on the bulletin board of the dorm, requesting a guitar player for a country music band. It was not my nature to push forward at all, but with the success of my last day in high school still ringing in my ears, I thought I would give it a shot. I auditioned and won a spot in the band. Soon we were playing for Grange meetings and various groups on campus. Then we got our own radio show and made some appearances on TV. It was so exciting that I changed my major to communications and eventually graduated in Radio and TV Speech. On what slender threads some of our major life decisions hang!

I had quite a few successes during my college years,

but deep down, the old nagging self-doubt kept rearing its ugly head, despite my accomplishments. Sunday meals were not included in our board bill at college, so I would often take the band to some of the sororities on campus. This gave us a free dinner with the girls, after which we would entertain them with music, a "sing for our supper" type of thing.

One day, during my junior year, I sat across the table from a very attractive young lady named Barb at one of our sorority visits. However, just after dinner, a 9-foot-10-inch tall good looking Rock Hudson-type football player came in and took that little doll out for the afternoon. So, giving up easily, as I usually did where girls were concerned, I made a mental note for some future time. Barb told me later her date was a 5-foot-8-inch folksinger, and that she came home that evening to phone her mother and tell her that she had just met the man she was going to marry—me, not the folksinger. I felt the same way, but I figured she was taken, so I just put her on the shelf with all my other unfulfilled dreams.

We met in May, and a month later we both attended a conference at a Bible camp near Seattle. Some might think it strange, and perhaps it was, for me to be constantly involved in church activities, and yet religion seemed to have so little effect on me. I was co-chairman of the event, so I could choose the committee I wanted to monitor, and I just "happened" to monitor the group in which Barb was participating. Then a tragedy occurred. My shoes got wet and I decided that I had better go home to Tacoma and get some dry ones.

"Barb, would you like to ride to Tacoma so I can get some dry shoes?" I don't know where that kind of courage came from. I wasn't sure how my mom would react to my having a *girl* in the car after midnight, when the closest thing to dating I ever had before was to take some chocolate chips to a girl named Jean when we were in second grade and brief flirtations with a couple of hired girls on the farm.

Barb and I returned to the conference grounds, were unofficially engaged by Friday of that week, and had our wedding planned. Once I got the hang of it, I guess I could move fairly fast. It was kind of fun.

Since things happened so fast, Barb and I decided not to tell anyone about our future relationship until we returned to school the next fall for my senior year. We hid the ring in her sorority mother's trunk when we got back to school because I couldn't find an evening to make the announcement, I was so busy. I was going fifteen different ways at once, just as I have continued to do throughout the years. I remember that one of my college professors took Barb aside one day during that final year and said, "Do you really know what you're getting into?" (meaning that people in the communications field tend to be very busy most of their lives).

Barb replied, "Of course," but she really didn't—nor did I, for that matter.

After the conference, I checked to see if I could take Barb home to Wenatchee. I had planned to go to Coulee City to work on the farm anyway, so I would just go a few days early—no problem! "Love to go! Not out of my way at all!"

We stopped at my folks' place to stay overnight before going across the mountains to Barb's home. My folks treated her as kindly as I knew they would. I can still remember that day very well. I was sitting in the living room and Barb appeared—in a *dress!* I had never seen her in a dress. Just think! I had brought a real live girl home to meet my folks, the kind I had read and dreamed about—perfect! Even after thirty years of marriage, I still get butterflies just looking at her. There have been lots of rough spots along the way, but

I know God gave me the perfect girl to be my wife.
We had a great trip to her home in an old 1940 Studebaker that my dad helped me fix up.

I have such a wonderful dad. He could fix anything.
He has saved everything he has ever owned or found
since he was four years old. He has a garage that the
Smithsonian wants when Dad is ready to give it up. He
has all kinds of exciting things in it, such as the left
rear throw-out bearing for a 1948 Jeep, the fanbelt for
a 1923 Model T Ford, a right rear fender for a Hupmo-
bile, in case they ever come back, a coupling for a 190-
ton air compressor, one of every nut and bolt General
Motors has ever made, and a spare 1932 Model A motor under the workbench. You simply never know
when someone is going to stop you and ask if you
have handlebars for a 1937 Harley motorcycle. I had
the time of my life among the treasures in my father's
garage as I was growing up.

My mom is also just about perfect. But one of her
few failings was that she wanted Dad to clean up the
garage. What would he tell the Smithsonian? Where
would he put everything? Didn't she know the stuff in
the garage was worth money? The proof of Dad's wisdom came every three or four years when he would
fix a faucet or a window latch or the furnace with
something he had saved since high school. Mom would
be so pleased to have it fixed, but I never really
thought she had a true appreciation for what would
have happened if Dad had not hung onto that particular bolt or screw.

And then there was the car. The what'sit made
noise, the muffler bearing was shot, the framas was
leaking. And what did my dad do? Why, he fixed it, of
course. Within just a few months he would get right to
it. He really was busy at the shop and didn't have time
to be coming home every ten seconds to fix Mom's
car. When he drove it (he would exclaim in a fairly

firm voice), it drove perfectly. It usually took just a few more months after the first complaint before both of them were in the car at the same time, so Mom could point out the various defects to Dad. The problems would then get fixed rather quickly once Dad discovered it was only the ringelnoffett rather than the grindandshafter. Lucky it was the ringelnoffett, because otherwise it would have taken a major overhaul.

One of the things Dad couldn't fix (Mom made him throw away the part) was a glove compartment latch for the 1940 Studebaker. When we would go over a bump, the door would clang down and bang Barb on the knee. Many times during the trip to her home after that Bible conference, I would hear the click, catch the door before it hit her knee, and slam it shut again. The opening and closing of the glove compartment made us late, so her family had already begun to eat when we got to her home.

Just as we drove up I heard this loud, raucous laughter coming from the little kitchen where the family was eating. I was sure they were laughing at me, and how in the world could I disappear without Barb noticing that I was gone! I got up courage and got out of the car and followed Barb into the house. It was a fairly small kitchen, and had 482 family members jammed into it—all Barb's relatives. Her dad was telling a joke (they told us later) and he wanted to get to the punch line before we got into the house. Anyway, after they quit laughing at me, I sat down to dinner with them.

Barb's mother is really strange. She fixed the oddest things to eat, like cooked broccoli, pickled beets, salad with string beans in it, corn on the cob, and other strange foreign dishes. I was a good old boy, who loved ham and eggs and biscuits with gravy. My first meal at Barb's mother's home included not only corn on the cob but *tea!*

Tea always reminds me of water torture, the kind where they drop water on a person's head until he cracks. There are other barbaric ways to destroy a man's mind. They take a man into a simulated back-yard and make him mow the grass and pull up weeds in the flower beds. His mind snaps within days. Another way is to put him into a simulated football stadium and have a continual half-time show of high school marching bands. They also put three or four people in a room and make them *visit*. There isn't a man alive who can stand that sort of punishment.

I found out very early in life that if I chewed six or seven rows from the corn cob, I could turn that side up, covering part of it with the salad lettuce, and it would appear that I had enjoyed my meal—until they started doing the dishes. By then it was too late. I had already left the table. I also found that if I put fifteen teaspoons of sugar in the tea, I could choke it down by holding my breath and taking small sips.

Anyway, I passed the test with flying colors. Often I tell Barb how corn and tea brought us together.

Two of Barb's small nephews began bugging me to go out and play ball with them. This would require leaving my precious Barb for a few minutes, but I knew my sacrifice would be good PR with her folks, so I got up and went outside with the boys. It also got me out of visiting.

Barb and I were married the following February and began our life together. After two days of marriage, I remarked to her as we were riding along in the car, "I wonder what all this adjustment talk we've heard about is, anyway." We had heard that there might be some pressure in marriage that would require compromise and fine tuning in our relationship. But since we had had no problems so far, that must just happen in other marriages, I thought.

After my senior year in college, I went into the army, and we ended up at Fort Bragg, North Carolina. I served my time in psychological warfare. I loved my job in the army. They were short of officers, and I, as a second lieutenant, filled the position of a major as training officer of a battalion. I guess a little confession is good for the soul, so I'll tell you that since I was training officer, one of my jobs was scheduling yucky things like the infiltration course where vicious trainers parted the trainees' hair with tracer bullets as they crawled through the dirt. I also scheduled the gas chamber exercise, where the trainers found who had the defective gas mask, and the field exercise where they were introduced to every gnat and fly in the area, and had to shave in cold water, using their steel helmets as a sink. Luckily I was trained in the Signal Corps, so I knew where the electric plug-in was on the generator and could use my electric razor. The generator made so much noise it covered up the noise of the razor.

But there's more. Since I was training officer, I also convinced the colonel that the weather would be much cooler for all of the above-mentioned exercises in October (which was true), and he agreed. One slight coincidence—I was discharged in September (I hope they don't make me take army over again, now that they know).

I really didn't understand the army anyway. I was supposed to be training people in psychological warfare, but it seemed someone always had me picking up pine cones, or straightening the lines in the dirt under the barracks, or policing (picking up) cigarette butts. So I decided to find my fortune elsewhere.

While we were serving time at Fort Bragg, we began to attend a church in nearby Fayetteville. It was there that a young pastor gave me my first glimpse of the joy that being a Christian could offer me. Before that time, I had the impression that the Christian life was something to be endured.

Barb and I were 11:00 A.M. Christians to begin with. Later we began going to a Sunday school class because of the overwhelming warmth of the young couples in the church. Then one of the leaders asked us to take a young people's group, called Jet Cadets, Sunday evenings. I remember so well thinking, *Just how much can the Lord expect me to do? Imagine! Going to church two times on Sunday!*

We had two children by then, compliments of the army. Thank you, taxpayers! Tim cost us $7.50 and Bev cost us $25.00. (Girls are much more complicated than boys. I think you knew that.)

I came out of the army with no job and with a wife and two kids to feed. One of the Seattle TV stations was going on the air a few months after I got out of the service, so we decided to wait and see if that opened up any jobs in my field. In the meantime, I worked in an apple warehouse and stewed.

Then one day Kit Spier from KING TV in Seattle called and offered me the chance to try out for a job as floor director. Talk about being excited! I was put to work setting up scenery, working with TV personalities, painting sets, cueing actors, and many other interesting assignments. At that time even a phone call from KING TV was an honor, since they were the top TV station in town. Because they were the leader in the field, they had long lists of people waiting for just about every job they had. Therefore, another person was competing with me for the position of floor director. I was excited to be given a chance, so I worked very hard at everything I did—painting, cleaning shelves, rearranging props—I even offered to do extra things, and not just to make points. I was thrilled to be there and liked to keep busy. The guy I was competing against evidently was not all that excited about doing the extra things or working too hard, and the reports I got through the rumor mill seemed to indicate that he complained when he had to stay a few extra minutes overtime or work on a Saturday. I accepted these things as routine.

We were doing a TV show at that time called *King's Ring*. The station would bring two or three boxing matches into the studio, using a huge ring made out of four by fours. Our carpenter always made things to last, even though the average length of a show was only a year or so. After the match was over, one of the duties of the floor manager was to empty the "spit bucket" the boxers used. I took that in stride with all the rest, but I'm told the other guy didn't really carry through on such disagreeable chores. When it came time to make a choice, I guess they picked the one who could empty the "spit bucket" best, for I got the job.

I remember my first full day on the job. There I was—a farm boy from Tacoma and Coulee City, standing beside a TV camera, with one of my idols just a few feet away—Charles Herring, *the* newscaster in the Northwest at that time. I was in shock for days. He treated me just like a *person*. I've always appreciated Charlie's warmth and good humor. We still have a close relationship. He was a very special person in my life because from him I learned to be a professional. I also appreciated the loving concern of Ted Bryant and Casey Gregerson, two people with whom I had gone to school. They had made it "big" on TV, yet they seemed to enjoy having me there. I guess that's one of the things I've learned over the years after meeting many "important people." That is, the *really* important people usually don't act like it. They are pretty common and unassuming. It's the folks on the way up that seem to have the superiority complex.

Anyway, I was impressed to be working on the news with Chuck Herring. One of my first jobs was to put the Alka Seltzer in Mr. Herring's water glass during the last news story before the commercial. He always led into the commercial by holding up the glass of fizzing Alka Seltzer. It was my job to make sure it was fizzy at the right time. The director of the show would take a close-up of Mr. Herring while I crawled into the set on my hands and knees, dropped a tablet into a glass of water, then crawled back out. One day the director got busy and forgot to cut to the close-up lens. I was new, and I didn't know a close-up lens from Mount Rainier, so I proceeded to do my usual thing. I crawled into the news set, only this time it was with the whole Northwest watching me. No, I didn't get fired—it wasn't my fault. But it did make an interesting memory for all of us.

I remember also the live commercial we did for a linoleum company, where we put on too much ink and grease and they just smeared when we went to show how easily the tile would wipe clean. And one of the announcers who was demonstrating "breakless" china, and it broke. And the "easy starting" lawnmower that never did start. And the announcer who leaned into the microphone after hearing a "wow" on a record, asked "Where'd you get that record?" then named on the air the name of the store he'd been told. It so happened that the next commercial was for that particular store.

Once we did a TV show at a manufacturing plant here in town. My job was to cue a Japanese man to pull a chain that would hoist a huge fish out of a tank. I carefully explained what he was to do. He nodded and bowed, so I assumed he knew what he was to do. Then went live, and it came my time to cue the fish person. I did, and nothing happened. He just nodded and bowed. I cued him again, but he again just

nodded and bowed. I found out later that he understood only Japanese, so we never did get the fish out
of the tank.

Another one of my TV idols was Stan Boreson, a
kid's show host. We hit it off right away in terms of
our sense of humor. I began appearing on his show as
a singing "Victrola." We wrote our own songs and had
a marvelous time. After I became a director, I was assigned to his show. We would meet about 3:30 in the
afternoon each weekday to prepare for a 5:00 P.M.
show, spend a while talking, laughing, planning, and by
5:00 P.M. we had a show on the air that seemed to ap-
peal to all ages. I took Stan's place on the air from
time to time during his vacations, which was a terrific
training experience for doing my own TV commercials
and programs later on. In fact, my whole experience at
KING TV was the Lord's way of putting me through
"school." I learned how to produce TV commercials
and programs as well as edit and direct film documen-
taries.

Then after a while I was moved into middle management, responsible for everything that was not "live," including program logs, announcers, films, commercials,
videotape, shipping, and a bunch of other duties. Actually I was shuffling a lot more paperwork than I really wanted, but I had a secure future with the company
and enjoyed my associations. However, on August 6,
1968, after almost eleven years on the job, the Lord impressed on my spirit that I was to hand in my resignation, because he had something else for me to do.

God didn't write on the walls, or speak out of the
clouds, but I knew positively that I was supposed to
leave.

I wrote out my resignation that evening, with no job
in sight, and with a wife and kids who still liked to eat
regularly. It was a bit difficult explaining to my friends
and co-workers why I was leaving. Not too many of

them understood what I meant when I said something about it being "God's will." Since I had no "message from the clouds," I couldn't really explain. I just had to leave—that much I knew.

I had taken Advertising 101 in college, so I thought maybe that would be my next career stop. I had never written a commercial even though I had directed the filming of many of them. I had never shot a foot of film myself, except for one church film I had done using a rented camera. All of a sudden, I was thinking about getting into a field where both of those skills were mandatory, at least starting out on my own.

While at KING TV, I had directed Safeway TV commercials for a one-man agency who had the account. The man was a little threatened by the sales department, so when he had a film or something he wanted to look at, he would sneak in the back door, come to my office, and ask me to help him run the projector or look at the slides. I was in another department at the time, but I always did what I could to help him. I had lunch with him after I left KING and asked if he knew of any advertising agency that needed help. He said he didn't know of any, but could use some help. So I went to work for him as his production director.

He was a fine, moral, honest man, and, humanly speaking, I owe my entire career in advertising to him. I learned much at his feet, but I was frustrated time and again by not being able to really please him with what I did. I would write some copy, but he would tear it apart, which was his privilege as boss. My goal was to please him, but I always seemed to fail. Then one time I took some of *his* copy from the previous year out of the file, typed my name on it, and he tore that apart as well. He just had a hard time letting go. It was good for me to find that out, because that way I didn't take his criticism so personally.

Everyone else seemed pleased with my work, so I

kept trying to do the best job I could for our clients, and grow in experience as well as mature as a person, even though I was miserable at times. Sometimes I would go home in tears and tell Barb that I just had to get out of there—go back to KING, go out on my own, pump gas, dig ditches—anything to get out of what I was going through. That was when I learned that sometimes we have to separate God's will from our emotions. I wanted to leave, but had no peace in my heart to go. It was almost as if God was saying, "Stick with it. I have some exciting plans for you later, when you go through this next phase of 'school.'"

In spite of my frustration, the Lord continued to help me to meet each day at the small agency. I began taking more and more responsibility and learning valuable lessons that I could apply later in my career.

One day, out by the elevator, the wife of the owner talked to me as I was preparing to leave work. She said that she and her husband wanted me to have the agency when he retired since they had no family of their own. He was almost at that age then and wanted to start taking things a little easier.

Then one Sunday afternoon I received a very strange phone call from the owner's wife, asking me to come to her house right away. I knew something was wrong, so I was not overly surprised at the news that the owner had died. As far as I knew, he left no will, so the promise of the agency died with him.

We tried a partnership between a secretary, the owner's wife, and myself, but it just didn't work. I offered to leave. Neither of the others had the background to carry on, so I bought the agency from the owner's widow and began to pick up the pieces and carry on, as the owner had wanted me to, only now I was paying for the business rather than having inherited it.

I was questioned by a number of people as to why I didn't just walk away. There was nothing to buy except a few typewriters and file cabinets. A service business really depends on a person rather than an inventory of equipment. I told them I felt an obligation to help the owner's widow since it appeared she had nothing except the house she was living in. And I think the Lord honored that decision. It was a good testimony to quite a few of my non-Christian friends.

I thought it was important to have a good testimony in my business, but I would have to say that Barb was far ahead of me spiritually. She always had been. She had not worked outside the home while the kids were small, so she had time during the day to read the Bible, which helped her grow. Since the Bible was still a dull, dry book to me, I simply went through the motions of being interested in church to please her and in a way to keep from disappointing my parents. I served on church boards, taught Sunday school and junior church, and was blessed in a limited way. But down deep, I was still a baby spiritually.

I realize that some people would say of me at this point, "Well, he wasn't really a Christian." But I don't agree. I *had* received Christ as my personal Savior, believed that he was born a man, that he was God, that he died and rose again, that he became the sacrifice for my sins, and that he was now preparing a place for me in heaven. I just didn't have anyone in my life who had the time, inclination, or knowledge to take me under his wing and help me grow by getting me into the Word. And I certainly didn't have those desires on my own, or if I did, I didn't have the tools to do anything about them. There is absolutely no doubt in my mind that I was a born-again Christian. I simply had not ever gotten into the Word, which was the spiritual food I needed to grow.

Barb continued to grow spiritually, reading the Bible and a number of Christian books she kept lying around. I tried to read a couple of these books, but it seemed as if the authors had their heads in the sand and could not relate to the world I had to live in. They talked about my problems, all right, but they gave me the impression, just as many of the pastors and teachers in my life, that they had it made, spiritually speaking, and why was it taking me so long to get to where they were? In other words, I felt they were trying to put me on a bunch of guilt trips. So I didn't read Barb's books, even though they probably would have been good for me.

I wasn't comfortable with things that were "good for me," like asparagus and the Bible. I thought I was fine just the way I was. I think Barb is amazed now when I come home all excited about a "new" book I've just finished reading. She walks over to the shelf and takes down the same book, brittle with age, about which she was excited ten years ago.

One day a friend of mine, George Toles, who now works with the Seattle SuperSonics, gave me a book to read. I could fake others out of reading Christian books and magazines, but I was afraid that George would actually ask me later how I had liked the book he had given me. So I figured I would have to read it, or at least enough of it so I could do the "part I like best" routine I used to do with book reports in high school and college. I tried several times to get into the book, would put it down for a few more weeks, and then try again. But then one day I finally made it past the first chapter of the book George Toles gave me, and what happened after that is a story in itself.

TWO
66 Reality 99

The book from George Toles stunned me. This author was reading my mail! My whole spiritual world began to open up. The book was Keith Miller's *The Taste of New Wine* (Word Books, 1965). Here was a man who seemed to be honest with his feelings. He actually said he failed once in a while. Can you imagine a Christian admitting that? He mentioned problems he was hav*ing* (not past tense). I couldn't believe it! Imagine a Christian who had problems, just like me! I consumed that book and immediately read his other three books that were available at that time. Keith said astounding things like, "Sometimes I don't feel God is very close," or "Sometimes I don't feel like going to church," or "Sometimes I don't feel like praying," or "Sometimes I want God to leave me alone."

What do you know? I had experienced those same feelings once in a while. And now there were at least two of us on planet Earth who felt the same way. But he didn't leave me there. He also told me how his life was filled with Christ, how the tears flowed so easily when he reflected on Christ's sacrifice for his sins, how Christ had given him a reason for living, the blue in his sky, the gold in the sunset. He had become like Christ and was God's own son too. I longed for that same closeness to God that Keith Miller talked about. I began my own search for the secret of his success in finding reality in life through Jesus Christ.

One day the man who maintained our ditto machine at the advertising agency stopped by to drop off some supplies. He shared with me some news about a speaker who was coming to town that summer to do a "Basic Youth Conflicts" seminar, whatever that was. I was not "into" seminars, especially a youth-type seminar. I politely told Harvey Edds that I wasn't interested, just to get him off my back. Harvey just kept smiling as I explained to him why I couldn't go to the Basic whatever-it-was. I was much too busy. Then he told me that it would take every evening for a whole week! That settled it for sure. I could never make time for that. "Thanks anyway, Harv."

But Harvey was not put off. He simply stooped to one of the lowest tricks known to mankind—he appealed to my ego. He casually mentioned that Bill Gothard, the man doing the seminar, was thinking about putting his seminar on TV, and needed someone to give him some "expert" advice on how to go about it. What happened after that brought about some of the most radical changes I had ever experienced in my life.

What Harvey Edds said turned out to be true—they were thinking about putting the Basic Youth Conflicts Seminar on TV, and needed someone to give them some advice. But I'm sure Bill Gothard could have found someone with a little more clout than a small-time operator from Seattle. But, of course, I *was* an expert of sorts, and might be able to help them out, since they needed help so badly.

I arranged some meetings with a few of the people involved, talked to Bill Gothard on the phone, and decided that the only way I was going to find out how to put this seminar on TV was *to attend the dumb thing—every meeting for a week!* "Lord, how much suffering can you expect a person to go through in a lifetime?" My back hurt during a thirty-minute sermon or a church committee meeting. But there didn't seem to be any alternative to going. Now you get the picture of the sneaky way the Lord and Harvey Edds worked. (Thank you, Harvey, with all my heart.)

I made plans to attend the seminar, and Barb, of course, was happy to go along with the "TV expert." Then I received a second shock. Not only was the seminar every evening Monday through Thursday—it was *all day Friday and Saturday!* I couldn't imagine spending that much time sitting, especially listening to something "religious."

I figured I could take some books to read. I probably would have taken up knitting if I had thought of it. How was I going to exist through that much preaching? But alas, I knew I was trapped into going, because they were desperate to have an "expert" tell them how to televise the seminar and I guess I was the only expert they could think of.

I noticed that there was quite a crowd of people who had been "conned" into signing up for the seminar. When I registered I was given a huge red notebook with blank pages for notes. Boy! Was it *red!* You could see someone carrying one under his arm ten blocks away. Maybe if I put my coat over it, no one would know where I was going. And fat chance I would ever take any notes! What a waste of paper!

Then Monday came, and Barb and I went into the auditorium. And what a shock to see more than five thousand people there, sitting in just about every seat, including a whole bunch of them seated on the floor close to the speaker. Imagine actually choosing to sit close to the front! Fortunately, we were way up in the rafters where I was a little more comfortable. I saw this tiny person way down on the stage, with just an overhead projector and a soft voice. "O Lord," I said, "this is going to be harder than I thought." But at least I could hide with that many people around, so he couldn't ask me to recite a memory verse or ask me to pray. On that first night my attention was directed toward finding suitable camera locations, and wondering how in the world I would be able to anticipate the audience reaction. They were actually laughing at some of the things he was saying! By Tuesday, I began listening to the speaker, partly because I couldn't escape, had no books to read, and because I hadn't yet learned to knit. But by Saturday night, my life was *changed!* I must have told this story two hundred times over the years since that first night, but my eyes still fill with tears as I think back on that breathtaking event in my life. As I sat there the rest of the week, my focus no longer was camera positions and audience reactions. My focus was Christ, the real Christ, the One for whom I had been searching for so long, with no real hope of ever finding him in a practical way.

I can't remember even a twinge of back pain as I sat for those thirty hours, soaking up this new practical message. I guess the difference between the thirty-minute sermons I had heard and this seminar was the simple fact that the seminar hit me where I lived, and most of the time sermons had not. From a spiritual standpoint, that was the most important week of my life.

I can't begin to tell you what an impact this event had on my whole person. It was almost as if I had found a small secret gate in a dark forest, and had the splendor of the universe suddenly unfold as I stepped through.

One of the most important things I learned was the fact that God owned me 100 percent. Prior to that week, the Lord and I had a 90-10 split. I would give him 10 percent of my time and money and I expected him to really be excited about my great generosity, since I knew some people who gave only a dollar on Sunday. Bill Gothard pointed out that God had paid a price (Christ) for me and owned me 100 percent, including my business, home, cars, bank account, family, time and tennis ball machine.

I guess I always had the impression before I started reading the Bible that Christ had marched to the cross with banners flying, anxious to pay the penalty for my sin. Now I learned that in the Garden of Gethsemane that fateful night, Jesus agonized in prayer, asking his Father that he not have to go through with it. Yet, he chose to do his Father's will. That made his sacrifice much more meaningful to me. How could I do any less than make myself a "living sacrifice" as my "reasonable service," as Romans 12 says?

Giving myself 100 percent to the Lord did not necessarily mean I had to sell everything and give it away. What it meant was that I simply no longer had ownership of anything. So if God allowed our home to burn down, our car to be smashed up on the freeway, my wife to get cancer, me to be crippled up in an accident, or for me to be a financial success, have a good business, perfect health—whatever he had in his plan for me—that's what I wanted to do or experience. That didn't mean I just sat on my sofa and waited for God to do something. Even though God owns the committed Christian, he still wants him to try doors, fill out job applications, search the want ads for homes, send kids to college, put savings in a bank, buy insurance, and plan for retirement. We can't just sit and assume

God will take care of everything without us just because we belong to him. He likes action. It's much easier for God to change our direction if we are moving than it is to get us off the couch. I believe in burglar alarms and fire insurance, not building fires in the middle of the living room rug, or lying down in the path of a speeding train. God's ownership means that after I have done everything in my power to do what God wants me to do, or to protect his property, and still something happens to it or my plans don't quite go the way I want, I accept the circumstances as coming from God to teach me patience, mature my character, or to give me the ability to love and help people as they go through similar struggles.

The second most important concept I learned that week was that the highest calling for a Christian was to be a servant—the highest calling. My natural self didn't want to serve. I wanted to be served. I wanted to be noticed, to be important, to have my name mentioned, to be honored, to be the first in line, to be president. A servant is usually not noticed. A servant is able to allow credit and honor to go to others, even for things the servant himself does.

This attitude of servanthood became the philosophy of my business. To work for clients as a servant became my goal, to serve them in ways they didn't expect or request. I wanted to give those for whom I worked the honor of getting the credit, even for some of my ideas with which they had nothing to do. I wanted to serve them just as Christ would if he were here in my place. I learned what a privilege it was to be a servant.

One of the most valuable lessons I have learned from Scripture is that love is an action, not a feeling. Many times I do not feel like doing the right thing for Barb, my neighbor, my boss, or my kids. But since I know God would have me do a certain thing, I do it as

an act of my will. An interesting thing often happens—
the feelings come, too. I've had some times in business
where the people in authority over me were unfair, demanding, inappreciative, and gave me the impression
that I would be tolerated only until they could find
someone else who could give them a better deal.

One day such a man made one more in a long series
of threats. I went home to Barb and we went for a
walk in the cemetery, sat on some rocks, and talked
over some things I already knew. But God reminded
me again through Barb that his plan could not be
thwarted by anyone. If I lost the client, God knew all
about it and had something better in mind. It was the
first time in my life I had hyperventilated—only a big
word to me until that day when my breath came in big
heaves and my heart pounded for no other reason than
the stress of the moment. I knew God had a plan and
was in control, yet my mind rebelled at the thought of
losing something for which I had worked so hard with
so little reward.

In that cemetery, I once again rededicated my life,
career, family, material goods, time, and future to the
Lord, assuming that his plan would be the best for me.
I also knew in my mind that God wanted me to honor
and serve that person with all the strength I could
muster. I began doing that by an act of my will, no
longer fearful of what he could do to me. He couldn't
do anything that God did not allow. With this remind-
er, I began to respect, serve, and honor that guy, and
do you know, he softened and began to honor me
back and we became good friends.

I may never know whether or not he ever became a
Christian. My job was to love him, right where he was.
And when I did, God gave me the feelings of love I
didn't have, going into the project. All I did was obey.
God did the rest. This was an amazing lesson that has
helped me face similar situations since then, and it

was just one more confirmation that the Bible does have practical insights on handling our day-to-day relationships.

I'm sure, as I look back on those hard times, I probably was radiating a resistant spirit to my friend at first, and it was resistance I got back—a reflection of myself.

I suppose there will always be that type of person around, so the sooner we learn to focus on our own attitudes rather than on the other person's shortcomings, the better servants we are going to be.

That week at the seminar was the beginning. The baby Christian, who had lived on milk, finally had his first taste of roast beef, and spiritual growth began in earnest.

The next important event in my spiritual life took place that same year. I saw, for the first time, the complete edition of *The Living Bible*. Its simple, down-to-earth language was easy to understand, so I began reading it. Now even the Bible began to make sense! Spiritual riches were beginning to cascade down on me at a dizzying pace as I read. I was limp with excitement. This *Living Bible* was of tremendous importance in shaping my spiritual growth and getting me started in a regular study of God's Word.

Back when the Lord and I were splitting my life 90-10, I suppose one of the things that made me a little fearful of giving God everything was some bad trip I thought he might lay on me when he got complete control. I had this vague feeling that I had better keep a little bit of control, so he wouldn't get me into too many bad situations. The worst possible thing I could think of was that he might send me to a foreign country to be a missionary. I'm just an old farm boy. My preference is ham and eggs, not monkey tail soup or fried cobra fillets, or chopped turtle shell with ant eggs for dessert. Or I thought maybe he would have me play my guitar in the Salvation Army band, or make me let my hair grow, wear thick glasses, and pass out tracts in the middle of the city, or worst of all, make me be a teacher or preacher. (I'm sure you can see now why I was so fearful.) On Saturday night after that week when I committed myself 100 percent to Christ, I told him I would be whatever he wanted. I knew he would give me the grace to handle whatever it might be.

There was one thing, however, that I told him I would never do—not in a million centuries. I would never teach. Most of my teachers, as I mentioned, were people who "had it made spiritually," who had no problems. I knew I could never live up to that high calling, and besides I had a soft voice. I got teary easily when something meaningful came to mind. And I hated lesson plans. I had a fervor and passion to make the Bible real and practical, but I just didn't think many people knew how to do that. In church I was taught such things as how the Jewish tabernacle was constructed, which direction the Jewish tribes faced in the Book of Numbers, when the church started, the attributes of God, the seventieth week of Daniel. But no one had ever made the Bible practical to where I lived during the week. I realize, however, it could well have been *my* attitude rather than the teachers.

Anyway, after I had given the Lord the news that I would never teach, he got really excited. He was *so* thankful I didn't plan to get in the way. He said that he *did* have some teaching he wanted me to handle for him. But since we both agreed that I wasn't a teacher, then any little success stories of people being touched through any of my classes would have nothing to do with me. It would have to be *him* and what he would do through me. So I began to teach, just as I said I would never do, and he has given me hundreds of opportunities to "practice."

Prior to that first week at Basic Youth, people were a pain, at least some of them. How often I would tell Barb that the world would surely be a wonderful place if it didn't have any people in it. For me, the old saying was surely true: "If you want something done right, do it yourself." I just didn't need anyone. I also had schedules for everything. I knew what I was going to do that afternoon, the next morning, the next year, and pretty much what I wanted to accomplish in the next ten years or so.

As God began my teaching ministry, he started bringing people into my life who messed up my schedule! I would be working on a very important project when someone would drop by with a simple case of divorce, cancer, death, or threatening suicide, and expect me to stop everything I was doing and relate to his problem. Then God began his softening process in my life with this phrase (and I don't know whom to credit for it): "Circumstances are temporary; but people are eternal." The only riches we will ever transfer when the Lord comes or we die are the people we touch for Jesus Christ. Everything else in time will be dust—our schedules, goals, systems, commercials, homes, cars, money—just dust. God began to allow me to love people, supernaturally.

THREE

66 She Never Does It My Way 99

Becoming a servant began to make a difference in my life at home also. I always wanted to be a good husband to Barb, and this takes time. Even though our kids are older, I still need to be seeking them out and spending some time with them. We need to support our local church, and that takes time. We want to keep in touch with our neighbors and friends, and that takes time. I need to go to conferences and seminars, get some reading done, and they all take time. It all boils down to asking myself, Is what I am working on at this minute the most important thing I could be doing? Am I working on something that I could delegate to one of my employees? But what if they fail? I realized how hard it was to release someone to make his own mistakes.

Priorities are a never-ending battle for me. They are not set in concrete—they need to be set in sand, as they are constantly under change, fine tuned according to the circumstances God allows.

Barb is such a great help to me in dealing with priorities. We were coming back from a football game one day and I was looking forward to going right home and getting into my "paint clothes," getting comfortable, and picking up a book, having dinner, or even having just a minute to breathe before the next crisis hit. I am usually about fifteen steps ahead of Barb when we walk, and I was that day, too—until she remembered that as long as we were close to the university, we should stop by and see someone who was in the hospital there.

I hate hospitals! Hurt people are there, and I don't like to see all those tubes and bottles and bedpans and stuff. I am foregoing the "privilege" of having a heart attack or ulcers or something that would force me into one of those awful places where the nightgowns are so drafty in the back. Besides, where in a hospital room am I going to put my desk, typewriter, file cabinets, and where would the secretaries work?

When Barb announced this hospital visit, all of a sudden I was the one who was fifteen steps behind, as my body screamed its resistance to this horrible idea. Now, let's face it. Visiting the hospital *was* the most important thing we could do at that particular moment—no doubt about it. But it took Barb as my completer to help me do the right thing rather than what I wanted to do.

I had never really faced the fact that Barb and I were different in so many ways, and I guess I pretended that I could handle it without being open and honest.

One of the things Barb did that bugged me was to interrupt when I was telling a story. I wasn't all that anxious to tell the story anyway. But with a certain amount of coaxing, I could be persuaded to relate the events as I saw them. I would begin to tell of an experience and all of a sudden Barb would cut in with a detail that I missed or had wrong. Now, I admit, I didn't always get the details straight, but I did get to the right ending. So what if I mixed up the camping trip to Deception Pass with the bike ride to Yakima, or said that Sally and Bill went with us when it was really Duane and Lenora? Little minor details like that were not important—it was the big picture or punch line that was important, and I always got that right—well, usually.

I took Barb's interruptions as a threat, reading into them something like, "You dummy, can't you even remember who went with us?" or "You fathead, it was Tuesday, not Wednesday." I found out later she had no such thoughts. It was not in her nature to think that way. I just took her interruptions to mean that I had failed again. After three or four interruptions, I would turn to Barb with no little irritation and suggest *she* tell the story. Barb didn't want to tell the story—all she wanted to do was add the details.

One evening during a family dinner at a restaurant Barb interrupted me one time more than I could stand, so I blew up—quietly. But Barb knew I was angry. She was shocked. I had made her feel she was "perfect" and now all of a sudden, I'm mad at her, and in public at that. How could this be?

Later as we drove home, I was hoping the incident would fade into history without a big confrontation, but it was not to be. Barb in her honesty wanted to talk about it. I've always shied away from conflict. In fact, I hate conflict. She wanted to know why I had gotten so angry in front of the family, and what in the world was wrong.

As I have grown, I have come to realize that Barb was not putting me down or suggesting that I was a failure. She just wanted to make sure the story was accurate. I wasn't aware at that time that most women are detail-oriented and most men are goal-oriented. I had a goal—to finish the story. Barb wanted to make sure we didn't leave out the important details on the way to the goal. The way we finally solved this, mostly for my benefit, was to consider ourselves a sports broadcasting team. I do the play-by-play and Barb provides the color. I would report that the runner "punches over the middle for five yards" and Barb would add that "this was the fifteenth time this season he had rushed for more than five yards on third down, and that his mother-in-law's name was Anne, and he banked with First Interstate." I now tell the stories— Barb adds the color.

That was the real beginning of my facing just how different Barb and I were. I knew the Scriptures said that we were "one flesh" after we got married. So it was obvious my goals would be Barb's goals, my vacation plans would be Barb's vacation plans, my interests would be Barb's interests. The fact is, she was and is a totally different person, with interests, goals, and patterns of thinking that are different from mine.

One of the things that made sense to me, for instance, was for us to divide our lives into "needs" and "wants," according to our goals. So, we *needed* a new camera, but we *wanted* a new rug. We *needed* a new tape recorder but we *wanted* some new drapes. We *needed* a new set of golf clubs, but we *wanted* a new sewing machine. We *needed* some new tools, but we *wanted* some new dishes. Do you see how the pattern works? It is very important to separate needs and wants in your life, and if your goals are your wife's goals, then everything works out great. One problem *can* arise, however, and that is if your wife might have a different opinion as to what are needs and what are wants.

Barb and I find differences in how we express our

feelings. I tend to hide my feelings. I guess that began in my earliest days at school when I was taught that "big boys don't cry." Then in the army I was taught not to have feelings, or at least to hide them. Then I carried those teachings into my marriage. It takes me hours, sometimes days, to find out why I feel a certain way. Barb knows immediately why she feels anger, fear, or whatever, and she wonders why I don't know instantly why I feel a certain way. But I don't.

When Barb was working in the office with me, around 5:00 P.M. every evening I would call across the hall to find out where she wanted to take me to dinner. The kids were gone and I didn't want Barb to have to go home and cook, so we would go out to eat. Then our daughter, Bev, came home from college and began taking over the office work. But I would still call Barb at home to find out where she wanted to go for dinner. Sometimes when I called she would already be cooking something. Evidently my voice would fall, or, in some way, I would give her the impression that I would rather go out than eat her cooking.

One day I came home as she was preparing a meal. I put my arms around her and asked something like, "Why are you working so hard?" This statement, coupled with the fact that I didn't eat any biscuits that night, convinced her that I did not like her cooking, and we had a big blow-up over that. I *loved* her cooking—always did and always will. I had no idea why my voice would fall or how I had given her the impression that I wanted to eat out rather than at home. I fussed and stewed all that night, mulling over in my mind how I happened to get into "trouble" and trying to sort out my feelings to determine why I felt the way I did.

The next day I called Barb and said, "I know now why I would rather go out." It was because we do our best communicating at a restaurant. At home we had kids and dogs and phones and TV sets and employees to distract us. But when we went to a restaurant, she was all mine, and we could talk and discuss things without interruptions. She understood my feelings, and with great "sacrifice" has agreed to go out anytime I want.

Another difference we have is that decisions are easy for me and harder for her. For example, Barb has a major decision pending that she should have made before she was out of sixth grade but she keeps putting it off. It is the decision as to whether she would rather freeze to death or burn to death. She keeps wavering back and forth on this decision, depending on whether it is winter or summer.

Barb and I are a team. In fact, the Bible instructs us when we get married to leave our parents and "cleave" to our mates. The original language for "cleave" means "glue." In God's eyes, we are one unit, and if we try to tear the two apart, parts of each would be left on the other. That is why divorce is so horrible. There is never a clean break, any more than one can separate two pieces of paper glued together without tearing and damaging both in the process.

Barb and I are different. I'm a dreamer and Barb is practical. I used to zap her with some big dream or goal without much preparation. Since she is practical, she can figure out everything that could possibly go wrong with my dream. I would take Barb out to dinner and present my fabulous plan to her, expecting her to get up and run around the table with glee because she was so excited. Most of the time, though, she just sat there with a stunned look on her face, raised her eyebrow, and began to explain why it wouldn't work.

Barb is not a downer, even though she says she feels like it sometimes. She is just practical, and I'm just a dreamer. So I don't always get all the details in place before I want to begin pouring cement, or buy the motor home. When Barb's eyebrow would raise, I would fail her by instantly becoming defensive, withdraw from the conversation, throw my dream on the junk pile, and pout. I have since learned that I was approaching Barb like a cement truck rather than like a butterfly.

I've come up with a little secret just in case any of you dreamers have problems in this same area. I began to write Barb notes as I started to think about a certain project or goal, presenting the entire picture so she could have the same time to think about it as I did. That way I didn't have the disadvantage of misreading her body language before she had a chance to really consider the idea objectively.

The Apostle Paul discussed the husband-wife relationship at length. He instructed the wife to "submit to your husband's leadership in the same way you submit to the Lord" (Ephesians 5:22). This sounds just fine to husbands reading this verse, but many get the wrong picture about what God's instructions are. We should read what Paul said earlier, where he instructed both wives and husbands to "honor Christ by submitting to each other" (5:21). In no way did God plan for the wife to do all the submitting. In fact, I put most of the responsibility for a happy marriage on the husband. The highest calling for a Christian is to be a servant, and that applies especially to fathers and husbands.

Paul wrote:

And you husbands, show the same kind of love to your wives as Christ showed to the church when he died for her, to make her holy and clean, washed by baptism and God's Word; so that he could give her to himself as a glorious church without a single spot or wrinkle or any other blemish, being holy and without a single fault. That is how husbands should treat

their wives, loving them as parts of themselves. For
since a man and his wife are now one, a man is
really doing himself a favor and loving himself when
he loves his wife! (Ephesians 5:25-28).

I remember our first interior house-painting project.
I decided to choose the colors, and so I painted our
living room a beautiful mustard yellow, our bedroom a
luscious blue (Barb says it was apple green). The kids'
room I painted a fantastic hot pink and the bathroom
lime green (Barb says vivid blue).

I found out later that Barb wanted her rooms white
(off white). She thought she could add color with pil-
lows and furniture. But every room the same color? I
had never heard of such an idea! I was raised painting
things different colors, usually the color of paint that
we had left over from something else.

The next time we moved, Barb asserted herself
enough to insist on picking the colors for our new
home. She had every room painted white (off white),
just as I was afraid she would do. But after she added
the red chair, the brown carpet, and the colorful pictures, it didn't look half bad—to my amazement. In
fact, I kind of liked it! The moral of this particular story is that men, for the most part, should stay out of
interior decorating. Usually the only taste men have is
in their mouths.

Only in recent years have I learned that our home is
the extension of Barb's personality, just as my work is
for me. If a faucet is dripping, Barb's "nest" is leaking.
To me, it is just a faucet. And I usually am not in any
giant hurry to get it fixed. It simply does not appear on
the list of my top twenty goals.

I started putting a goal list on the refrigerator for
Barb. And she would put projects on the list, such as
gutters, faucets, garbage, leaves, and filters—which
seem to fill our every waking moment—and I would

cross them off as I got to them. Since none of her goals made my top twenty, this was an invaluable way for me to read her mind and help her keep the nest in shape.

It used to bother me to see how different Barb and I are from each other. I took these differences as a threat. No matter what I said, Barb would have another opinion, usually just the opposite of what I was thinking. When we went into a restaurant, I might comment on how good the coffee was just as she was thinking how bad it tasted.

Barb likes butter, but I prefer margarine. She is people-oriented, while I'm goal-oriented. She likes soft gentle music, while I like loud country music. She likes a variety of food, while I like the same old things all the time. She forgives easily, but I sometimes find it hard to forgive. She's optimistic, but I'm a pessimist. The list could go on and on.

There are obvious physical differences between men and women, but in addition, we are emotionally and biologically different. I recently read that a woman's brain is "wired" differently than a man's, giving her a completely different outlook on life. One of the major problems with the "women's lib" movement is that its proponents seem to be trying to make men and women the same. We will *never* be the same even though we can be *equals*.

Many times, before the wedding, the man brings his girl flowers, opens doors, talks, visits, shares feelings, but the day after the wedding, he turns again to make a living, build a career, watch football, play golf or tennis, and pays much less attention to his wife.

Since the man is usually goal-oriented and has accomplished a goal (finding a wife), he is now off to greater things. But she is left behind, emotionally shattered because the flowers and soft talk have evaporated.

Most of the time, men do this in ignorance, not to make their wives miserable. Husbands don't go to school to learn how to be good companions. It seems logical to most men that once they have found a mate and captured her, they can then go toward other goals. But a man can be *taught* how to be sensitive to a woman's needs. We have seen many relationships transformed when the husband begins to learn how to meet his wife's needs emotionally and spiritually.

I've always been the spender and Barb the wise saver and this difference in our makeup has been quite evident in some of the financial investments I have talked Barb into making. I would hear of something in which I thought we should invest, present it to Barb, and instantly her practical mind began punching holes in my dream. She would say strange things like, "I don't trust that person," or "I don't feel good about that project." What did feelings have to do with investments? I knew who I could trust. I knew that all the numbers had come together logically. I felt we should go ahead with the plan. Besides, I'd worked with that person for a couple of years. What did she mean, "trust?" He'd never let me down before.

After sensing that I was determined to do "my own thing," Barb would release me to do what I thought best, even though she was against it or had doubts about it. I would even feel as if I had to go behind her back on occasions, because I *knew* she would be against it. I didn't do this to hurt her—it was just that I was so sure I was right.

But, do you know, as of this writing, I am zero for six in terms of succeeding with projects Barb felt were not right, or with persons whom Barb did not trust. I would be kicked off most sports teams with a won-lost record like that, and I guess that's just the point. I had gotten off Barb's team. I think one of the problems I wrestled with was that I thought understanding meant agreement. When Barb and I would have a little conflict (sometimes a big conflict), she would say, "You just don't understand me." And I would say, "You're right!"

I found out later, however, that was not the answer she needed to hear. In fact, that is why she would come at me nineteen different ways with the same thing. We would talk about something, and—what do you know—the same subject would come up a few weeks later, but from a little different angle. I would say something like, "I thought we talked about that," or "Why do you have to bring that up all the time?" The reason she kept bringing up the same things over and over was that she didn't think I understood her feelings on the matter. And sure enough, I didn't, because I thought I had to agree with her, and I usually didn't.

I learned that understanding just meant reflecting Barb's feelings back to her in my own words. I didn't necessarily agree. For instance, we used the envelope system for our finances when we were first married. We would divide our take-home pay and put so much into the food envelope, so much into the clothing envelope, and so much into the miscellaneous envelope. Near the end of the month she would say, "I'm just about out of food money." My usual response was, "You'll make it." What I should have said was, "I'll bet that makes you uneasy, doesn't it." "You worry about the kids having enough milk, don't you." "Thanks for taking our finances seriously." As I became the mirror to her feelings, she knew I understood. All she wanted was for me to be sensitive to how she felt.

I don't seem to be able to keep communication going when I'm confronted with something. I tend to defend myself, which only makes things worse. Much of it has to do with my temperament and the way I am emotionally designed. I can choose to grit my teeth and communicate at the height of emotion but I fail far more than I succeed. What Barb desperately needs is for me to understand her feelings, accept her for having feelings, and not show disapproval for her getting emotional. This is such a hard area for me, but I'm working on it. She wasn't looking for instant solutions—she was looking for understanding. What I needed to learn is called "active listening."

The principle of active listening is useful in all our relationships, with kids, bosses, neighbors, and especially wives and husbands. I went to an assertiveness seminar not too long ago to find out the difference between being assertive and aggressive. We as Christians can become confused on this issue since the world keeps telling us to do our own thing—think of number one, if it feels good do it—that sort of thing. There *are* times when Christians need to assert themselves. Too many people think that Christians should be doormats. On the other hand, there are times when a Christian should give in, yield, surrender. Simply put, I learned that being aggressive means to run over people with projects or goals, not taking into consideration or even caring about their feelings in the matter. Being assertive, on the other hand, means that I want the other person to know how I feel about something, but also I want to know how they feel, too. It is an even-handed approach.

During the seminar, we had an exercise in active listening. We paired off with another person whom we did not know. The idea was to pick something on which we disagreed from a list of subjects. The seminar was secular, so there were many subjects to choose from, such as abortion, women's lib, Trident, ERA, and living together outside marriage. Each person was given two minutes in which to convince the other person of his point of view on the chosen subject. We could do anything except slug the other person. We could yell, threaten, intimidate, or pound our fists on the table to make our point. This we all did, and the room was bedlam. Then we did another exercise where each person would state his case and the other person would simply listen, and then reflect back the other person's feelings, not their own. Person A then confirmed to Person B whether his reactions were correct with regard to how A felt. Then Person B presented his or her side with Person A listening and reflecting back the feelings and thoughts. I saw people even switch sides as they, for once, were listening rather than just thinking about what they were going to say next. Practicing this principle in relationships may transform the way we deal with many of our struggles.

Early in our marriage, Barb and I had always been pretty much in agreement when it came to helping other people or spending money on big projects or investments. We began to tithe during the first year of our marriage. God honored that commitment, and he has never once failed to meet our needs. Something would come up that involved money. We would discuss it, ask each other what amount the other person had in mind, and most of the time we could independently come up with the same amount. This was one of the ways God confirmed his will to us. This happened too many times to be just chance, so we were certain God had a hand in our financial giving.

Now, I realize that the smartest thing a husband can do is to take his wife's counsel, especially if the project involves relationships of any kind. That doesn't mean she is always right or that the husband always has to do everything the wife says. If the project is really God's will, then the Lord is quite able to soften the wife's heart and give her the trust and confidence to look to his leadership.

Suppose the wife *is* wrong in her counsel, and they don't do something God would like them to do. I would suggest letting God take the responsibility for that. We shouldn't step in and cloud the issue. I would rather leave something undone than strain our marriage team.

One of my biggest failures, past and present, is stretching Barb too much. For instance, when we moved into our present home, I *really* had some big plans. I figured with this big house we could easily handle groups of at least a hundred. In fact, one hundred fifty would be better. All Barb had to do was a little dusting before the guests came and rig up some dessert of some kind—no big deal. I found out later that she had different expectations. She had dreamed about entertaining couples or singles—people who came through town and needed a place to stay. Here I was, all of a sudden, inviting the entire town of Tacoma over for lunch! The first clue I had that I was pressing her too hard in our new home was the time I was teasing my sister-in-law about our plan to have the University of Washington marching band over for some tea that weekend, and Barb *believed me!*

One evening Barb and I started out to go to a basketball game and stopped at a restaurant on the way. Barb began to cry and couldn't quit. She *wanted* to quit but couldn't, she was so stretched and tired.

I can just hear all you wives saying, "You beast!"

And you're right. I guess I was, but I didn't mean to be so insensitive. I was just ignorant of what Barb was feeling, as she did her best to support me in the things I was planning. I really failed her. Even now I'm not as sensitive to her needs and energy level and goals as I should be. I need to learn what Barb needs to help her grow and provide it for her.

When God appointed man to rulership in the home, he surely didn't mean "dictator." He meant "servant." It takes work, attention to detail, unconditional love,

God's help, and a great deal of prayer. The bottom line of marriage is that it is a lifetime commitment.

Some men might think that their marriages are too far gone to recover now. Let me suggest unconditional love as the remedy. We mustn't base our love on the performance of our mates, but on knowing that God wants us to love. After we love our mates by an act of the will, the way God wants us to do, then the feelings will follow. God keeps his promises. We have to do our part by not dwelling on the negative, but by thinking of the good things. We can rejuvenate troubled marriages and neglected relationships. It's well worth the effort.

FOUR
"God's House"

For many years, beginning with the day Barb and I were married, I had a very special dream house in mind. It was a Southern Colonial, with pillars, weeping willows over the drive, a deck off the bedroom where I could pad around in my jammies, the privacy of acres of woods, a front porch with a rocking chair, looking out onto a peaceful front yard.

There was only one problem. Barb didn't really like Southern colonial homes with pillars. And there was no way I could insist because in preparation for a young married's Bible study I was teaching, I found out that the home was the extension of the woman's personality, and the business is the extension of the man's. Because I learned this principle, I had to let Barb pick out our home. However, I kept working on my list of wants in a house, only now it was not a Southern colonial with pillars.

One of the reasons for the dream home was to have room to entertain traveling missionaries, teachers, pastors, and friends as they came through town. We had actually been doing this all along, squeezing them in among the family, which was not all that bad. But how nice it would be to give them a private room with a bath and give them special treatment, in an elegant setting! *The Living Bible* speaks about how Christians should take guests into their home, show them hospitality, and send them on their way with a gift:

Dear friend, you are doing a good work for God in taking care of the traveling teachers and missionaries who are passing through. They have told the church here of your friendship and your loving deeds. I am glad when you send them on their way with a generous gift. For they are traveling for the Lord, and take neither food, clothing, shelter, nor money from those who are not Christians, even though they have preached to them. So we ourselves should take care of them in order that we may become partners with them in the Lord's work (3 John 5-8).

Every once in a while, I brought up the subject to Barb of moving to a larger home. But she didn't seem too interested. We had a nice home and there was very little motivation for her to leave. We did have some minor conflicts with a lady next door with whom we shared a driveway, but this was not pressure enough for us to move. Then an angry dog moved in behind our home. Every time we would let our perfect puppies out into the backyard, this dog would raise a fuss and begin fighting with them through the fence. I squirted him with the hose once in a while, but decided this was not a good way to maintain a Christian testimony with his masters, who never seemed to notice the dog's bad attitude.

Then a fine family with seven boys moved out of the house on the other side of us, and some young, hippie-type people moved in and began playing their loud rock music. We would wake up at 3:00 A.M. with our bed vibrating to the bass notes. Cars raced up and down the street all night. There was an occasional loud fight outside our bedroom window, and we would find empty six-packs in the rose bushes the next morning.

I'm a little threatened by this type of people, but Barb had the courage to approach them. They seemed apologetic, but the beat went on. The next time I brought up the subject of moving—strange thing—Barb thought it might be something we should look into.

I had been talking with Dan Tradal, one of our Christian friends, a real estate salesman. He thought, from a tax and investment standpoint, we should find a bigger home. Since Barb was now agreeable to a move, I gave Dan the description of my dream house. Several items on my list made him smile, because they were things that made it impossible to find such a place in Seattle. But I gave him the entire list of requirements anyway, just for fun. I was amazed! He actually wrote the items down: close to the city (I don't like to commute); spiral staircase; lots of different rooms; privacy; grounds that wouldn't take too much work (I put lawn work somewhere between having bamboo shoots pushed under my fingernails and being forced to walk on hot coals barefooted). I also needed a room for my audio studio; lots of storage because I collect things; room for a tennis court; a view of the mountains; and a place for a home office or den. The things that killed the deal were privacy with room for a tennis court and close to the city—all impossible parts of the dream because there just simply would not be that type of house available.

Dan called a couple of weeks later with a house for

us to look at. We went to see it—guard at the gate; rooms like the White House; an acre of manicured garden. It just wasn't us. And besides, the guard at the gate would discourage people from dropping in, and since our son, Tim, was a mechanic and proud of his greasy clothes, the guard probably wouldn't let him in.

A couple more weeks passed and Dan called again. One of the homes near Seattle that I had seen and liked from the outside was for sale. It was a white colonial on a large piece of ground, quite run down, needing lots of work, and a little further out of town than I really wanted, but it *did* have room for a tennis court. On seeing it, I said, "No, Lord, I don't think this is the home you want us to have." I just felt that I would know for sure when we found the house the Lord had planned for us. Maybe he just wanted us to stay where we were, since we hadn't found anything yet.

Then one day, as I was riding in my car, listening to Kay Arthur's tapes on prayer, I was reminded of the verse: "The reason you don't have what you want is that you don't ask God for it" (James 4:2). Since I had never really been specific with God in prayer before, I thought I would practice. I prayed something like: "Lord, you know the dream house I have in mind. You know we want it to serve your people, so I pray right now that you will give us the home even today. And, by the way, as you know, we're still missing that sound track for our film [I did missionary films at that time and had been searching everywhere for a sound track we were missing—the lab couldn't find it, and we had searched everywhere]. You know I can't finish the film until I find that track. You know where it is, so I ask that you'll allow us to find that today, too." That evening the lab called and said they had found the missing sound track.

When I returned to my office, I found a note from

Dan saying he had found a home that he wanted us to look at. The time on Dan's note was *before* I had prayed, which brings to mind the Scripture that says, "Remember, your Father knows exactly what you need even before you ask him" (Matthew 6:8).

I called Dan. The price he quoted made me smile. It was well over what we could afford. However, we thought it would be fun to see a home in that price bracket, so we made an appointment to see the house. It was right on the bluff overlooking Lake Washington and the mountains. We drove down a long tree-lined driveway, past a *lighted tennis court* (I had forgotten to ask for lights), past a swimming pool (I didn't even have a swimming pool on the list), past a fountain in front of a beautiful brick home with four acres of natural woods surrounding it, right in the heart of the city. Right by the swimming pool was a separate little house with a living room, fireplace, kitchen, bathroom, dressing rooms, and storage rooms—an ideal place where groups or individuals could fellowship after a day of tennis and swimming, play guitars and sing, without disturbing the neighbors. Then we went into the main house itself, with the spiral staircase I had asked for, and into a "dream kitchen" (according to Barb), with an upright barbecue and a breakfast nook overlooking a spectacular view of water and mountains. The dining room was beautiful, with lots of windows looking out on the green outdoors and flowers. The seven bedrooms were breathtaking, and six baths ample for our simple needs. Barb, in her practical way, was looking around for the garbage cans. I made the comment that people living in a house like this didn't have garbage.

I was ready to buy after seeing the first floor, but Barb reminded me we had to have room for the audio studio. On the way to the basement level, we went by a complete office setup where I could make my headquarters when at home, a storage area where we could keep Barb's jars, canning supplies, and extra food, and a huge storage area where the furnace and pool filter were located—lots of places for my junk. My pulse was 120 by then.

The upstairs included a place for Barb's art studio and sewing room, a study and a wood-paneled library-den with a fireplace (one of four), a bar we could use for milkshakes and pop. Downstairs we discovered a fully equipped film studio with rewinds, projection screen, and film storage—a perfect setup for our missionary film activity. We walked through another door and came into a room that was the ideal size for the audio studio, even built out from the rest of the house so there would be no noise from footsteps up above—absolutely perfect in every way! The three-car garage would give me plenty of workshop room, and the greenhouse I forgot to ask for would give Barb room for her flowers. The treehouse for our guests' children was next to a set of swings in a beautiful little park-like area, which also included a covered sandbox. There was even room for horseshoe pits. The swimming pool had a bubble over it so we could swim year-round.

The property had a wire fence around most of the four acres—perfect to keep our puppies in and yet give them room to roam around. By the way, there was also a double kennel with a dog run. That's not so strange—the Lord knew we had two dogs.

It was a nice dream. The Lord had shown us a home with everything on my list—everything I could have thought of in my dream house and a whole list of things I didn't even think about having. We knew it was the one he wanted us to have, but our answer was, "Lord, we can't afford that much. So, please work a miracle if you want us to have this house."

We gave the house to the Lord, knowing it was his, but not knowing how he was going to provide the money to pay for it. We had made it quite plain in our own minds and to the Lord that if our ministries to people's financial needs, doing missionary films, supporting our missionaries, or local church work would be harmed in any way by a new house, forget it! We would live in a tent if we had to choose between a new house and our ministries, even though the house *was* going to be used primarily for his service.

When we left the property that day, I knew that we had just seen the Lord's home for us, but it would be a first-class miracle if it ever came to pass, a feat right up there with the parting of the Red Sea.

I stopped the car at the top of the little hill at the end of the lane and Dan, Barb, and I prayed that the Lord would allow us to buy this home. We asked the Lord to help us confirm in our own minds the price he would have us pay for the home as well as the amount of the down payment. And wouldn't you know (when you're dealing with miracles), we all independently came up with identical figures. "Now, Lord," we asked, "how are you going to pay for your house? It's still a lot of money."

A couple of weeks passed. The phone rang. A large company in Seattle asked me to consider taking their account, a client that had been the target of every advertising agency in town. For them to call me was a miracle in itself. The way one usually chooses an agency is to put out the word that you are looking, choose ten finalists, then seven, then five, then three, then two, then the winner. Here I was, being asked to take the account and I had never met one person at the company!

I found out later that one of our friends in the media world had given us a good recommendation. He's a wonderful guy, but I doubt whether he really fully understands he was working for God in that project.

When Barb overheard my conversation with these people, she began dancing around the office. She knew that was the answer—the house was ours!

In effect, the Lord had agreed with us that we should not disturb our other ministries with a large house payment so he provided a new client to help pay the bills—just another routine miracle.

We began negotiations on the price of the house with the owner's agent. We still didn't feel we could pay the full price the owner wanted nor handle the large down payment, so we made an offer—the full price, but no interest. It wasn't surprising that the owner rejected it out of hand. Following the rejection of our first offer, Barb, Dan, and I had lunch and discussed this "death of a vision." We realized that many times the Lord will allow things to "fall through" to help us grow spiritually as we lean on him for guidance. I was ready to accept the seller's full price, knowing the Lord would provide the money through our new client, even though we did feel the property was somewhat overpriced.

Barb felt we could do better on the terms. Barb and I make a good team. She tempers my dreams with facts. The facts were simply that we could not easily handle the full price the owner wanted for the house.

I have a tendency to jump into things. I remember the first house we looked at in Seattle after my doing time in the army. We were looking for a house with a large recreation room where we could entertain our friends. We began searching and found a nice home with a huge recreation room, milkshake bar, lots of space—just perfect. Except we didn't have peace about it. We prayed, but still didn't have peace. But we made an offer anyway—dumb! We had no business going ahead of God, but we did, even though we were not comfortable. Then a lady came to the owner and offered to pay cash for the house, and of course her offer was better than ours, so we were released.

After God bailed us out, we began looking for another home to buy. We were riding around with a real estate agent one day and he wanted us to see a home on which the contract had just fallen through. He thought it might come on the market again, and wanted us to look at it. As we drove up, another agent was just putting the "For Sale" sign back up. It had not even been placed back on the market. We looked at it, had perfect peace, and bought it. It makes tears come to think about it, because it had much more space and potential and charm than the other one. It was underpriced, needed some fixing up, but we had lots of time. It was a treasure and it was ours. It proved to be a perfect home for sixteen years.

We had another interesting experience with our office building, too. I had a downtown office and decided that since I always called on the clients at their office, and since the salespeople would find me anywhere I had my headquarters, I would try to find a building near our home to avoid the waste of time commuting. There were lots of advantages to being close to home. I got in the car and began driving around the neighborhood looking for an office to rent or buy. I noticed this small home situated on a business street in a commercial zone. I stopped in and found it to be perfect for what we wanted. I talked with the owner and said that I wanted to check it out with my wife, but that we were very interested in buying it. I told Barb about it, how perfect it was, and went about my business. Barb stopped by a little later to look at it.

I can't remember if it was that afternoon or the next day, but I got back to the owner after hearing from Barb that she also thought it would be perfect. The owner said it was sold. I was a little shook, because I was so sure the Lord was going to give us that little house for our office. I was disappointed, but I gave the office project to the Lord, and began driving around the neighborhood again, looking for something else to buy or rent. When I got home, I told Barb the office had been sold. She said, "Yes, I know. It was sold to *me.*"

She knew we both liked it, so she told the owner we would take it. It was as if God was testing me to see if I would blow up and get upset at finding out the building had been sold to someone else, especially after my being so sure it was ours. I was beginning to learn his principles and had just passed one of my first tests.

I thought perhaps the same thing was happening again with the "dream house." We left our lunch with Dan Tradal with no further plans. However, late that day, I called Dan and suggested he present another counter offer, this time the price the Lord had given us the first day we saw the house. I had a feeling our new offer would probably not be accepted either, so I filed all the information I had been gathering about the house in a "new home" file. I thought we had found the home God wanted for us, but evidently the Lord had different timing, so I put it out of my mind.

I had been so sure about our new home that I had been making lists of missionaries, teachers, pastors, and lay workers we would invite to stay with us for "rest and recreation." I had also listed all the things to do to get ready to move, notify the gas company, change the address at the post office. I was also making a list of things I would do to our new home—put a cover over the tennis court so we could play in winter, put in more security lighting, and clean out the greenhouse. All these notes and lists I now put into the "new home" file. I felt that even if we would hear on our counter offer, it would be quite a few weeks before the owner reacted. I thought our offer would probably be considered ridiculous and an insult to the seller because it was so much lower than what he was asking.

It also came to my mind that Sun Myung Moon and his followers were buying up lots of property, as were the Arabs. So to presume the seller would not receive an offer greater than ours was really silly. How could we have been so sure? We found out later that a young Arab did make an offer, but we were told that his father wouldn't send him the money.

We also found out later that a family of twelve wanted to make a "blind" offer on the house the day after we signed our earnest money agreement, and that offer was for the full price. The Lord has a sense of humor, because the woman who made the blind offer turned out to be the mother of the young men who had helped "motivate" us to move from our other home by playing their music so loud.

In our prayer time, we prayed for the seller himself, that his heart would soften and that he would be open to our terms. We also knew that he was a human being with needs and hurts like everyone else, and we wanted somehow to make contact with him to see if we could help him in a personal way, even if the house deal fell through. At that time we were dealing only with his agent, and we were driving her nearly crazy.

After we made our second offer (which was the price the Lord had given us the first day), the agent felt that it would not be accepted and wanted us to make another offer. Dan explained as best he could that the amount we were offering was all God wanted us to pay for the house, and we had to stay with that figure. I can just imagine the frustrating conferences in that real estate office as they talked about the "weirdos" who were acting and talking as if the house were already theirs. The day after I had begun filing away all the "new home" information, Dan called to say the seller was beginning to come down on his price.

I had been teaching a Bible study on Friday evenings, and what a neat group it was! Many in the group had been praying we would get the dream house. Several had even gone to the property and were convinced this was the Lord's house for us. One girl "claimed" the house for the Lord. How would she react if we didn't get it? That was more God's problem than mine, but I was concerned. I was playing a tape for the Bible study one Friday evening. The tape finished just as Barb was called to the phone. Barb came back and announced that the Lord had given us the house, at the price the Lord had given us that first day. Everyone cheered.

That same evening, Dan came over for us to sign the contract. Everyone cheered again as he shared how the Lord had led him step by step in the transaction.

One of the most meaningful things to me that evening was that no one in the group showed less than complete joy at our getting the house. There would be a natural tendency for at least one person to wish they also could have a house in that price range or have it handed to them by a miracle, but as far as we know, no one felt that way.

Later, one of the women who attended the Friday Bible study was talking with people at a Bible bookstore called The Bridge, sharing with them the miracle of our home. They were thrilled, because their Bible study group had seen an article in the paper about the house, and had "claimed" it for the Lord, long before our deal was firm and without knowing we even existed. The day after we moved in nearly a hundred people attended a dedication service. We invited the group from The Bridge to join us. We had a fantastic time sharing what the Lord had done, and everyone enjoyed seeing this miracle firsthand.

Sometimes we don't have because we don't ask. I'm not saying everyone will get the home of his dreams just by asking for it. But if it will be used to honor God, and it is his will for you, consider it done. God is not through working miracles yet!

FIVE
"I Boggeth Down around Noah"

Every now and then, for many years, guilt pangs would force me to take the Bible down from the shelf, blow off the dust, and try once again to make it meaningful to my life.

Since it was a book, I thought it was logical to start at the beginning, so I would start in Genesis—and bog down somewhere around Noah. It simply was not relating to where I lived, so I put it back on the shelf. Then the next time the guilt pangs came up, I would turn to the New Testament. Right away I was in trouble because Matthew started his book with a bunch of "begats" and "begans." Again the Bible had no meaning, so it went back on the shelf.

No one seemed able to make it come alive for me. I had learned isolated verses of Scripture during my growing up years, but these had never meant anything special. I had a vague feeling that I was supposed to

sit down next to some guy on the bus, spout off John
3:16 at him, and he would fall on his knees and receive
Christ. It never quite happened that way.

Then the time came when I attended the Basic
Youth Conflicts Seminar, and among other things, I
was introduced to the principle of memorizing whole
chapters of the Bible instead of just isolated verses
where the context is not always clear. I also learned
what it meant to meditate on God's Word. Meditation
had always been a bad word for me. I could visualize a
bunch of monks in a monastery chanting, "Ooo-ugh-
em-wowee-yum-look-o-phoey-youee-to-u."

I'm not into chanting, so I didn't think I would be
very good at meditation. I learned, however, that meditation was simply repeating back to God his own
words from the Bible. As we memorize Scripture we
just repeat the message back to him, and as we do, his
principles become a very real part of our lives.

The more we saturate our minds with biblical principles, the more we will react as Christ would when we
encounter bad situations. Our ways are not God's
ways. When someone curses us, we want to curse
back at him. But God's Word says, "Bless him."

Part of my problem in not understanding the Bible
was because I had been trying to fathom the King
James version, which was the only translation I had.

Now please don't get me wrong. The King James is a
wonderful version, and God has changed countless
lives through its pages. Some people will not use any
other translation, and that's great, but for me, I needed
things simple in my own language. The King James is
really only "Good News for Seventeenth-Century Man."
There is nothing sacred about the words *thee*, *thou*,
and *verily*, for that is just how folks talked in the days
when King James lived.

What an exciting day it was when I discovered *The
Living Bible!* My first reaction to being able to under-

stand what the Bible was saying, I thought, would be to pick out those items that I could apply to my Monday through Saturday life and put those few limited principles (maybe one or two per chapter) in a book that I could give out to my friends who were having the same struggles I was having in getting into the Bible. Or I could type out those isolated principles on a piece of paper, and pin them up on my bulletin board at the office so I could refer to them from time to time. Since the Old Testament was basically about the Jews and the Gospels were basically for the disciples, I decided to begin my own personal translation in Romans, since Paul was the missionary to the Gentiles. As far as I could figure out, I was a Gentile, whatever that was.

In order to sort out the items I would include in my personal version, I began underlining with a red pen those principles that I could apply to my everyday life. I was stunned! To my amazement, the pages began to drip red ink. In some cases, I was underlining almost every sentence in the chapter. And when I hit Romans 12, I just about came unglued because there were some *practical* guidelines for my life. I needed to give myself to God as a living sacrifice—not be caught up in things of this world, be a new and different person as a Christian. God's ways *do* satisfy. I need to be honest as I estimate my abilities. Each one of us has a special part to play in the body of Christ. God has given us certain gifts to use for him. We shouldn't just pretend to love others, but really love them. We should hate what is wrong. We need to delight in honoring one another. We should never be lazy in our work. We should be patient in trouble. We need to help out God's children. We should invite guests home to dinner. We should share each other's sorrows. We should not try to act big and important. We shouldn't think we know it all. We should not pay back evil for evil.

We shouldn't quarrel with each other. We should never avenge ourselves. We should feed our enemies. We should conquer evil by doing good—fantastic! Those were principles that hit me right where I lived!

Obviously I found out quickly that I didn't need to make my own personal translation, because I would have just been copying *The Living Bible* word for word. One of the things that I learned was that the *depth* of my message (getting into the Word of God) was my responsibility and the *width* of my message (ministering to other people who come into my life) was God's responsibility. And that is exactly what began to happen. As I started to put my nose into the Bible, I would look up and there was somebody who needed exactly what I had been learning, the exact same principle that was at that very moment impacting my life. So I would share the principle, put my eyes back into the Book, and look up later to see ten people there, then eighty, then hundreds, needing the very same things I was learning—principles that made sense and could be applied to everyday life.

After I completed underlining a *Living Bible*, I would buy another one and start over. I found that each time I went through it I underlined passages I had skipped the previous time. I bought *The Living Bible* on cassette tape so I could listen in my car. I had a copy of it at the office—in fact, a stack of them so I could give them away. I had a copy in every bathroom at home, in my office, in my car, in my briefcases and other places where I could get to them whenever I had a few minutes to spare.

Looking back, I guess one of the things that had helped to keep me *out* of the Bible was the judgmental attitude of some of the Christian leaders in my life who made me feel that I had to spend an hour each morning reading the Bible or I wasn't spiritual. I found out that for my life-style I had to get what I could in

bits and pieces during my busy day. I would read the
Bible when I found myself early for a meeting, or de-
layed in traffic, or waiting for someone at a restaurant.
It became the focus for my spare minutes. Everytime I
make a lunch date or schedule a breakfast, as I seem
to do five or six times a week, I take along the Bible
or some other Christian book that I am reading. I take
along my Bible and books when I go out, and when
people don't keep their appointments or get caught in
traffic, I have a terrific time reading and learning.

Last year I made an early breakfast date with a guy
who wanted some counsel, and against my real wishes,
found myself driving a long distance to make the appointment. I usually have a stack of things on my desk
that I just have to get done for the Lord, Safeway, or
Sears. But here I was, driving miles out of my way just
so this person didn't have to get up early or drive too
far himself. I know this is all part of being a servant,
but sometimes I think we can ask the other person to
put himself out just a little, especially when it is for
his benefit.

That day I had agreed to meet the person at a restaurant located about midway between Seattle and Tacoma. I got up early that morning to make the trip,
and it had snowed. I hate snow! Don't ever pray for
snow; my old nature would make me hate you, because I hate snow! Snow disrupts my schedule, makes
me put on funny tires with nails in them, and prevents
me from getting out of my driveway. I've seen some
misguided folks put long colored sticks on the roof of
their cars and head for the mountains. They really
must enjoy putting on tire chains and being miserable,
but I hate snow! Yuck on snow! Boo on snow!

So that morning I see I am in trouble, but knowing I
have to meet this guy, I go out in that miserable stuff
and put on those dumb tires, and bang my frozen
knuckles on the bumper jack that is always welded

down underneath the spare tire, which is always covered with stuff that I keep in the trunk.

I finally get those stupid tires on so I can get out of the driveway and begin the tortuously slow drive with all the jerks on the highway who haven't driven in snow since the winter of '23. They spin their tires and do sideway flips on the freeways at sixty miles an hour. I enter this madness to meet this fathead who made me drive one hundred miles out of my way to have a stupid breakfast where he probably won't take my counsel anyway! I have a telephone in my car, which is about the only thing that made sense that morning, and after I had almost completed the five-hundred-mile trip to the restaurant, it rang. I was informed that this guy had called and cancelled the breakfast because of the snow, after I had driven a thousand miles to keep the appointment! "Lord, how much suffering can you expect one person to take?"

Well, I looked for the next exit, slid into a restaurant parking lot, slushed my way to the door, flopped down in a cozy booth, had a nice refreshing cup of coffee, put on my glasses, and began to read one of the books I kept in the car while eating a nice warm meal, all by myself. And I learned a principle through my reading which I shared the following Sunday in the class Barb and I teach. Three or four people came up to me after class to say that what I had shared was exactly what they needed to get them through that next week.

Circumstances? Chance? Coincidence? Not on your life! That little episode was God-designed to test my patience, help mold my character, force me to stop for a few minutes to learn a principle he wanted me to teach to some other people who would come into my life later on. I would have blown the whole thing if I had gotten angry and asked a bunch of "whys."

It might be that trying to pick up scriptural principles in bits and pieces in restaurants, bathrooms, and

briefcases won't work for others. Maybe they need to
get into the habit of spending a certain amount of time
reading each morning or evening. I don't think it really
matters to God. I really feel he will bless our efforts
no matter what method we use to begin studying and
applying his Word.

We need to remember to approach the Bible in a
balanced manner. For instance, I have talked with people who try to appropriate every Old Testament promise into today's living. I have also been exposed to
people who almost throw out the Old Testament and
spend all of their time in the New Testament. Some
study only the letters of the Apostle Paul, some only
Paul's prison epistles. I think our answer is given in
what Paul wrote to Timothy:

The whole Bible was given to us by inspiration from
God and is useful to teach us what is true and to
make us realize what is wrong in our lives; it
straightens us out and helps us do what is right. It is
God's way of making us well prepared at every point,
fully equipped to do good to everyone (2 Timothy 3:16,
17).

Someone once asked me how I would go about
trying to reach a person who doesn't believe the Bible
is true. I don't think it can be done, humanly speaking.
All we can do in that case is to hope they will be open
to books and tapes that will explain the Bible better
than we can. Until we have a common ground, using
the Bible as the final authority, it is almost impossible
to have a meaningful discussion. Unless the Holy Spirit
is at work in the person's heart, nothing will happen
anyway.

I've learned it doesn't help to get into long, drawn
out discussions with people who don't want to grow.
Christ even suggested to his disciples to "shake the

dust off their sandals" when they found a city that was not open to their message or where the people didn't have teachable spirits. I run into quite a few people I call "Yes, butters"—"Yes, but I don't have time," they say, or "Yes, but I don't understand the Bible," "Yes, but I don't feel like it," "Yes, but she did it first," "Yes, but you should see the way my boss treats me."

I've told a few people that I could no longer help them, because of their unteachable spirit. I say, why bang your head against a closed door when a hundred doors are flapping wide open, people anxious, hungry, willing to learn and grow? It doesn't make sense. We can waste a lot of time feeling guilty when we should just turn to the doors that are open. It's essential, however, that we are into the Bible on a regular basis so that our message is growing.

People ask me, after their being exposed to all the denominations, cults, splinter groups, etc., "How can I know which one is right?"

Fortunately God has sent his Holy Spirit to minister to us as we read the Bible, and he will help us come up with the correct interpretation as we use the various tools available to us for study—commentaries, translations, dictionaries, word study books. I suspect people who draw the wrong conclusions about various Scripture passages have simply not gone far enough in their investigation. Most of the time they take only a cursory, shallow look at the meaning and can easily jump to the wrong conclusions by not comparing verse with verse and taking into consideration the cultural aspects of that particular passage.

It amazes me to hear people say, "I don't believe the Bible," or "It's full of myths and tales," or "It isn't practical to my life," or "I can't understand it." The reason I'm amazed is that most of the people who say things like this have never read the Bible, or at least have never made an honest attempt to see if the things in it are true.

I took astronomy in college. When I learned about Saturn's rings, it would have been stupid of me to say to the teacher, "I don't believe it. That's just a fairy tale," and then quit the class without looking any further. It is like saying, "I've never seen the rings, so they don't exist."

A very intellectual student was said to tell his Christian instructor: "I could never go along with Christianity because of the lack of credible evidence and the myths on which it was founded."

The wise teacher didn't put the student down or get angry or make him feel uncomfortable. She just told the student she would be excited to review the details of his research, since he obviously must have examined the basic documents concerning Christ.

The student said, "You mean, the Bible?"

"Yes," replied the teacher. "It goes without saying, that we have to investigate carefully things like this before coming to the conclusion they are false."

The student had to admit that he had never read the Bible. He joined the crowd of people who are critical of the Bible and yet have never read it, talking about the myths of the Bible, and never taking time to see if they are right or wrong.

After thousands of years of challenge, the Bible has proved to be true and accurate in everything it has claimed. Such a record is a pretty good indication to me that God *was* the author, not man. And even if I didn't have all this evidence about the accuracy of the Bible, I would have to consider it a supernatural book because of the changes in lives I have seen it make. First of all, the change in my own life is something no one can argue with. Second, there are the changes in the lives of the people all around me, men and women who seem to have changed almost overnight after an encounter with Jesus Christ.

One of my favorite stories is about a couple named Larry and Kathy Cyphers. I first met Kathy at the Safeway store where I picked up the TV props for my commercials. She was always helpful. I guess she knew I was a little "different," and her boss had mentioned something about my being a Christian. I can't remember ever talking with him about it. One day Kathy's sister-in-law, Sandy, mentioned me as being the teacher of a Sunday school class at a church in the north end of Seattle. Sandy had been attending the class and invited Kathy to join her. Kathy's first question was, "Can I wear my jeans?"

Sandy said, "Sure."

So she came. Later in the afternoon on the day she came for the first time, Kathy and Sandy went out to pick berries, and Sandy had the privilege of leading Kathy to a personal relationship with Christ, right there in the berry patch.

Immediately Kathy's life began to change. Kathy and Larry were divorced at the time, yet they would see each other once in a while. Larry saw such a change in Kathy that he decided to attend the class pizza party one night to see what kind of "cult" Kathy had gotten herself mixed up in. He came with a wall of resistance built up around him. He was amazed to see the people laugh. No one flopped a Bible in front of his face. And they ate pizza, and didn't wear their hair in a bun or wear long dresses! It wasn't long before Sandy was instrumental in bringing Larry to the Lord too. And he began to do strange things, like read the Bible, and his life began to change. A few months later they were remarried in our home, and now they are teaching and loving people all over the place, helping to change lives in the same way God changed them—through his Word.

If there were no other evidence of the Bible's power than a changed life, I would still have to accept its supernatural influence.

Another thing I run into once in a while is a non-Christian who finds it difficult to figure out why God had to become a man to save us. When I worked on a farm during the summers, I used to go hiking in the sagebrush, looking for petrified wood. Every once in a while on my travels, I would run across a giant red ant hill. I would always take some crackers and bread along to feed the birds, so I would stop and crumble some of the crackers or bread around the ant hill. Those ants would go out of their minds with this manna from heaven. However, as I observed the ants, I saw that they were not very smart. Two ants would argue over the same piece of crumb. I would see others go way out of their way to get back to the nest. I would see ants struggling to climb rocks with bits of bread when they could have gone around the rocks much easier. I could have shouted, blown horns and sirens, stomped my feet, threatened them, rung bells, but there was no way they would even know I existed. Even if I stepped on a few of them, there would be no understanding of what happened.

The only way I could take a message to those ants would be to become an ant. If my message made sense, they could relate to me as an ant and take my advice. The only way God was able to bring a message to us was to become one of us. The Bible is the account of that encounter of man and God (Christ), so it is essential that we read the Bible to find out how this encounter can have an effect on our everyday life.

I never thought I would ever come to the place where the Bible would be anything but a dull dry book. But I stand amazed at God's gift of understanding as he touched me through the Bible. I pray often that my experience will help others get into the Word.

For me it has never been completely convenient to study the Bible, and I'm sure that Satan isn't that anxious for any of us to begin. He has all sorts of other things for us to do, but we have to keep at it, and make time for it, even if we think we don't have time.

Reading the Bible reminds me of the words "can't" and "won't." People say, "I can't exercise, I can't diet, I can't quit smoking, I can't quit drinking, I can't discipline my children, I can't get along with my wife, I can't get the dishes done, I can't get to church on time, I can't remember to clean the gutters, I can't clean up my room, I can't understand the Bible, I can't pray, I can't get anything out of this lesson."

But the real truth they should be saying is, "I won't exercise, I won't diet. . . ."

What we do or don't do involves our priorities. We get those things done that are important to us. We may forget the dentist appointment, but we hardly ever forget the tennis date. We forget the committee meeting at a church, but would never forget the aerobics class. Our priorities indicate our values. The way people can see what is important to us is to observe what we do.

But priorities can change. It takes constant readjustment and fine-tuning. Right after I left KING TV and began working in the small advertising agency, I was involved in producing Christian films for various organizations—missionary films, camp films, and slide presentations. I worked long hours on these and other projects. I think they accomplished some good things for the Lord. But as I began getting into the Bible on a regular basis, and my message began to deepen, God began to trust me with people. He began to bring all sorts of hurting people into my life and started phasing out my film ministry. By staying close to his Word, I sensed this adjustment in my priorities and began to spend time in this new direction.

I could have continued to do films. There was and

still is a need for this type of service. But God had something better for me to do. Our priorities speak so loudly they drown out our words, and one of the priorities that will have a maximum impact on our lives is the priority of Bible study. One begins studying the Bible through an act of the will. Then God begins his work of shining his searchlight on the Scriptures being read and maybe for the first time in our lives, we too will be excited and blessed as God's Word and instructions come alive before our very eyes.

It wasn't always like that for me. But because I began, I can now say, "Thank God for the Bible and its message about the love of Christ—an unspeakable gift."

SIX

"Why Me, Lord? Why Now? Why This?"

Barb just came down to the office. "Are you writing? A fuse blew," she said.

It's because of the crummy roof gutters that the fuse blew. We have some workers here fixing them and they needed to plug their drill into the fountain outlet where the circulating motor froze this winter, next to the broken stonework that someone crushed with his car, by the storm drain that is plugged with leaves. Leaves also plugged the gutters which caused the problem in the first place or the workmen wouldn't be here.

It doesn't bother me one bit when little trees begin to grow out of the gutters. In fact, I kind of like the effect. It makes a nice wind break, a kind of frame effect around the edge of the house. Barb doesn't see it that way. She wants the gutters clean.

Barb has a real thing about leaves. We have 9,856

leafing trees around our place and every autumn, they "leaf" all over our driveway and yard. Now my thought—a logical one, I'm sure you will agree—is to wait until all the leaves have made their way to the turf. Then we take our little rake, do the pile of leaves bit, and get rid of them. But Barb has this funny idea about raking several times during the season. In fact, each leaf or seed pod, as it clicks and lets go of the branch and flutters to the ground with a thump, she can hear from anywhere in the house. At that point, she wants someone to go out and rake it up, or clean them out of the gutter, thereby depriving innocent little trees of life.

Barb doesn't like moss either. We have some bricks on our patio where mosslings gather for picnics and family outings. After a few months the brick begins to take on a green hue, as the mossling families grow in number. Barb's idea is to destroy all these innocent things, creating all sorts of trauma. I destroy them, but not without guilt pangs as I destroy such innocent creatures.

Now maybe you don't wrestle with leaves, or gutters, or mosslings, but I can imagine you have other things in your life that cause you to suffer—and we don't want to suffer—at least, I don't. Suffering is the last thing I want to do. I want things to go smoothly so I can do all the things I want to do, not all the things I have to do. I hate to have things happen that are out of my control, like too much rain, snow, death of a loved one, loss of a job, an earthquake, or other trage-dies.

As Christians, we realize that suffering is part of the Christian life, even though that is not how we would have written the script. Sometimes our natural response to suffering and trials is to assume that God doesn't know about them. Trials have all kinds of ben-

eficial things for us, two of which are found in the
Book of James:

*Dear brothers, is your life full of difficulties and
temptations? Then be happy, for when the way is
rough, your patience has a chance to grow. So let it
grow, and don't try to squirm out of your problems.
For when your patience is finally in full bloom, then
you will be ready for anything, strong in character,
full and complete* (James 1:2-4).

These verses show that trials are "when" and not "if."
Trials *will* come, no matter how hard we pray or how
many times we go to church. They are inevitable.

My question is usually, Why? These verses show us
the purposes for trials and suffering. The sooner we
accept that trials are inevitable and that they have a
purpose, the sooner we'll make an impact on the people around us, especially our non-Christian friends.

When non-believers see Christians handle their struggles and trials the same way the world does, they
question why they would need Christ in their lives. If
Christianity doesn't make a difference in the way we
act, who needs it?

If our attitude is Why me? our focus is inward—not
outward. We need to get on top of our circumstances,
not let them get on top of us. When we are on top, we
can see the big picture as God sees it. But when we
are under our circumstances, all we can see are the
problems, the struggles, the pain. What we need to do
is thank God for our trials, assuming that he has a purpose in allowing us to experience them.

I have scores of media salesmen calling on me in my
advertising business. I have to learn to trust these people as people before I can trust what they tell me
about their station or product. The better I get to

know them, the more I can trust their product. I know some of the salespeople so well that I would trust them with anything. That's the way our relationship with God needs to be. We have to get to know him so well that we can trust him to have a purpose even when problems come. And the only way we can know God is by saturating ourselves in his Word.

Some of my problems result from being unable to do all the things I have planned. One day after lunch I dropped by an electronics store to pick up some tapes. (My secretary tapes the Chuck Swindoll radio program every day, so I can listen to the tapes in the car as I go about my business. I'm usually about a year behind in listening to the tapes, but that's OK. I'm being fed spiritually while I wait for red lights and traffic jams.) When I got back to the car from purchasing the tapes, the car wouldn't start. I tried and tried, but no go.

Sometimes I fail God at such times by asking something like, "Why? Didn't you know I was in a hurry?"

However, as I've gotten more and more into his Word, I'm able to give the situation to him, as I did this time. I was grateful that the car had not stopped on the freeway or on a bridge, or when I had a crisis appointment. It was a very nice car—one I used for my business. As it was, the car was in a parking spot on the street. I had an afternoon with no real crises, so I put some money in the meter and walked back to the office, which was only a few blocks away. I was thanking God for the situation, assuming that whatever he had planned was OK with me.

Later that afternoon I had the car towed home, and the rest of the week, I drove a small pickup truck we have for the business. I'm just a farm boy anyway, so driving the truck was no big deal—it was fun. Two days later, I noticed I had scheduled a lunch with a brand new Christian who repaired appliances for a living. I drove to his shop, went inside, and instantly realized why God had stopped my car. The guy had greasy clothes and would have been very uncomfortable riding in a luxury car in his work clothes and probably would not have been able to relate to me very well because of the car. But he was at home in a truck, since he drove one every day. We had a fantastic lunch, sharing Christ with each other, building each other up, having a great time. I returned him to his shop and drove off in my little truck with at least a hint of why I had the truck that day rather than my regular car.

When I see Christ face to face, I'm going to ask him, "Did you really make my car stop so I could drive the truck to see my friend?"

He may say, "No, it was just your PCV valve," but I suspect he will say, "Yes, you see, before the foundation of the world, we knew you would be having lunch with your friend, and knowing that he would be threatened by a big car until he got to know you, we just decided to stop your other car for a while and let you drive the truck."

From God's viewpoint, my inconvenience was a thousand times less important than having lunch with my friend. God is just that practical. I thank him so much for a beautiful verse which says, "We can make our plans, but the final outcome is in God's hands" (Proverbs 16:1).

We once had someone working for us whom we discovered to be dishonest. I had every reason to march into the office, ask the person to leave, and to make restitution for the wrongs done. But I didn't have peace about doing that. So I prayed, "Lord, I know you want _____ to leave, and so do I, but I'll leave the timing up to you."

Several weeks went by, and evidently God was real busy in Africa or Asia, because he had not done one thing about my problem. So I took the problem back from him and wrestled with it on my own. I could hardly be around that person, because I was so suspicious and uneasy and worried. Then all of a sudden I realized that I had taken the problem back. It was God's problem. So once again I prayed, "Lord, I know you want this person to leave, but it's your problem now." This went on for several months until one day in desperation I prayed something like, "It's a real mystery why you haven't caused this person to leave. Could it be that you want this person to stay? If so, please help me to accept your will in this matter. I really do want to please you—not myself."

In two weeks the person was gone. A situation came up which caused this person to leave the city—no confrontation, no bad feelings. When I completely turned it over to God he answered—in his own time, which was perfect.

There are other reasons for suffering and trials besides those that mature us and build our character or teach us patience. Paul wrote about it to the Corinthians:

What a wonderful God we have—he is the Father of our Lord Jesus Christ, the source of every mercy, and the one who so wonderfully comforts and strengthens us in our hardships and trials. And why does he do this? So that when others are troubled, needing our sympathy and encouragement, we can pass on to them this same help and comfort God has given us. You can be sure that the more we undergo sufferings for Christ, the more he will shower us with his comfort and encouragement (2 Corinthians 1:3-5).

Time after time, as Barb and I take couples out to dinner and begin sharing some of the problems we've had in our marriage, the other couple will say something like, "That happened to us last week. What do we do about it?" Then we are able to relate some of the practical lessons we've learned through various situations and from reading Scripture, and offer them the same comfort God gave us in those circumstances. The longer I live, the more I can see that God brings into our lives people who can benefit from the lessons we learn by going through problems.

I have had only two people come into my life in a teaching or counseling situation who have had cancer. Since I've never had the disease, all I can say is that I will pray for them, show sympathy, visit them in the hospital, and try to help in any way I can. But I can't say, "I know how you feel," because I don't. On the other hand, when hurting couples come to us with a marriage communication problem, I can say, "I know how you feel," because Barb and I have experienced that kind of problem many times. There is no doubt about it—wounds and scars do qualify us to counsel.

We need to share hurts with each other; especially those of us who teach must be open and honest, sharing present-day problems as well as those we have put behind us.

We can be joyful through the tears when we run into problems and trials. As our patience develops and our strength grows, we learn to trust God more each time we go through a struggle. The stronger we become, the higher we can hold our heads, no matter what happens, or how deep the tragedy, or how painful the trial. We know that God loves us and will not allow anything to come into our lives that is not in our best interest. He goes through the problem with us, because his Holy Spirit is right there inside us, filling our hearts with the knowledge of God's love. But we can't trust someone we don't know. We can't even trust God if we don't know him, and we can't know him without getting into the Bible on a regular basis.

Barb and I have gotten to know a number of professional athletes here in Seattle and around the country.

We see behind the scenes how hard they work before the cheers begin. They punish their bodies, making them do things they don't want to do—run, lift weights, run, do pushups, run, work out on the Nautilus equipment, run, sweat, and run some more. The world really doesn't expect to see Christians work hard. People have some idea that Christians are "pantywaists," sissies, or pushovers. But Paul wrote:

I'm not just shadow-boxing or playing around. Like an athlete I punish my body, treating it roughly, training it to do what it should, not what it wants to. Otherwise I fear that after enlisting others for the race, I myself might be declared unfit and ordered to stand aside (1 Corinthians 9:26, 27).

From these verses we can see that a Christian *should* run his or her race to win, to gain first place in business or athletics, to be the best homemaker possible, the best neighbor, the best church member, the best pastor, the best truck driver, the best advertising agency person, running with purpose, setting goals, eyeing the mark, denying self, being the best Christian he or she can be.

Time is too short to play games in the Christian life. We have to either get on the ship or get off the ship. We can't have one foot on the dock and one foot on the ship and expect to go anywhere. We can straddle only so long. Some of us have too much of the world in us to be comfortable with Christ, and too much of Christ in us to be comfortable in the world.

I used to work with a man who acted, sounded, and looked like a Christian when he was with a Christian group. But when he was in a social situation with non-Christians, he acted, sounded, and looked just like one of them. The non-Christians in his life knew he should not be involved in some of the things he was doing, yet I suppose it gave them some comfort to drag him down a bit.

There are other reasons for suffering, and these we don't like to talk about. Sometimes we suffer for doing wrong. If I go seventy miles an hour on the freeway and get a ticket, I deserve the ticket—I did something wrong. It surely doesn't make much sense for me to grouse around, mumbling against God for bringing this "suffering" into my life. I simply have to pay the consequences for my sin, then get up and go on.

I know quite a few people who are suffering for the wrong they have done, and are getting impatient with God. It's almost as if they want God to start over, to erase the consequences of their sins. We should pick up and go on after we blow it and not look back, after having asked God's forgiveness (and that of any people involved). But that does not mean that the consequence of adultery, divorce, stealing, or lying will just go away automatically when we get our behavior straightened out. There is a price to pay for sin, and the best thing we can do is be patient and let God work out his will in the situation.

We sin because we are tempted to sin, and because we didn't resist the temptation. God does not let us be tempted beyond what we are able to stand. However, he doesn't "set us up" for failure. I feel that once we invite an evil thought into our mind to play with it for a while, God takes off to Korea or Africa and leaves us on our own. In effect, when we toy with temptation, we are saying, "Don't call me, God. I'll call you."

Satan knows exactly what makes us tick and where we have weaknesses. If we have a tendency to steal, he will make sure we have lots of opportunities to steal. If our tendency is for lustful thoughts and actions, he will make sure we run into all kinds of TV shows, movies, and magazines that will help feed this weakness so that the thoughts lead to actions.

Nobody fishes with a hammer tied to a string. The fish would laugh at that. To fish we put a wiggly, fat, juicy worm on the end of the line and pretty soon we've got a fish. That's what Satan does to us. He doesn't waste his time in the areas of our strengths. His favorite fishing ground is with our weaknesses, and he begins his subtle work in our minds. If *Playboy* and *Showtime* are our daily mind food, then our minds will be sensual. If the Bible is our daily food, then our minds will be spiritual. There may still be an occasional battle, but if we're properly nourished, God can help us win the struggle. Someone said that a dusty Bible results in a dirty life, and I know from experience that is true.

I once visited an aluminum plant. The heated metal is pushed through a specially shaped die and out comes the aluminum shaped as gutters, molding, angles, or rods, according to whatever die was placed in the machine. As Christians, we get heated up a bit with trials and struggles in order to make it easier for God to push us through the die to make us what he wants us to be. How much pressure and heat is needed to push us through God's machine to make us like Christ? As with the metal, just enough to overcome the natural resistance of the material being molded. What this says to me is that the more we fight or resist, the more pressure and heat God has to exert in order to mold us into the image of Christ.

As we deal with struggles and problems, sometimes we may not know why they happen to us. However, God often shows us the reason for a particular trial after we have gone through it. When we face difficulties, our natural tendency is to give up and quit, but God's Word says just the opposite. When I read Paul's phrase, "We get knocked down, but we get up again and keep going" (2 Corinthians 4:9), it reminds me of those little inflatable dolls with lead in the pedestal that makes them keep popping up when they are knocked down. God's Word encourages us:

So take a new grip with your tired hands, stand firm on your shaky legs, and mark out a straight, smooth path for your feet so that those who follow you, though weak and lame, will not fall and hurt themselves, but become strong (Hebrews 12:12, 13).

One of my chores on the farm was bringing in the milk buckets from the barn. They were heavy, running over with fresh milk, and once in a while I would have to stop and take a new grip on the handle in order to make it. Even though it seems this passage in Hebrews is talking mostly about getting up after God has had to discipline us, I think we can use the same principle with suffering and trials. For sure, some of my problems are a result of God's trying to get my attention.

God *does* discipline his children as needed—every loving father does. However, God's discipline looks to the future as he helps us back on the path—not back at the past, but at the road ahead. Paul reminded us that "these troubles and sufferings of ours are, after all, quite small and won't last very long. Yet this short time of distress will result in God's richest blessing upon us forever and ever" (2 Corinthians 4:17). So, difficulties are used by God to make us better or more useful.

We all want to be used for Christ's highest purposes, but we have to be the right kind of dish or vessel. I once read that in some archeological digs in Greece, they found clay pots with the Greek word *dokimas* stamped on the bottom. The word means "approved," meaning that particular pot went through the kiln and didn't crack under the heat. It was given that stamp so that people would know they could put their best olive oil or wine in the pot and it wouldn't break. What a beautiful picture of what we should be for God—a vessel uncracked, proven through the fires of struggle and trial, fit for God's best purposes.

God doesn't put us through the fire to see when we'll crack. He puts us there to temper us and make us strong so that we will be ready for anything that might come along.

I also look at myself as a channel, wanting to be clean and pure so God's love can flow through me to the other people in my life. If I'm contaminated with anger, bitterness, lust, or jealousy, then I block God's love from flowing through me to others, so I can't have the effect in other people's lives that God would want me to have. Suffering is not something I enjoy or look forward to. But it does help me grow and make me more valuable as I share God's Good News with the people he brings into my life to love for him.

A number of suffering people have asked, "When will it end? I don't see any light at the end of the tunnel. I can't stand any more. I want it over. Why is this happening to me?"

I've searched the Scriptures and I can't find any promises that our problems will ever end until Christ returns or we die. The purpose of trials is to help us grow. What's so wrong with growing? It hurts, but who has our best in mind? God. What has he promised? To see us through our problems. The results he seeks have eternal purposes, if not to prepare us better for life on earth, then for life in heaven.

In a shop class in high school, we made chisels as a class project. We put them into the fire to temper and harden them so they would be prepared for the hammer blows later. In the same way, God puts us through the furnace of adversity to make us ready for anything. Someone has said, "God doesn't use someone until he has allowed him to hurt deeply." Part of this tempering process involves being a servant. A servant is one who does the will of the master, no matter what he is asked to do. God may be saying, "I want you to grow through this sickness. I have another person who will come into your life later who will need the same comfort I am giving you now."

As God's servants, we need to do the things he wants us to do, when he wants us to do them, how he wants us to do them, where he wants us to do them— even if what he asks is for us to suffer.

I used to take my children to the shopping mall to "drive" around the empty parking lot. They would sit on my lap and we would drive all over the place. Sometimes on the back roads I would let them hold the wheel. But they weren't driving—I was. They didn't seem to notice that I had my hands on the wheel also. I guess they were too busy watching for cars and keeping in the middle of the road. When we would get home, they would bound out of the car and announce to the neighborhood that they "drove the car!" The neighbor's kids would grouse around, wondering why they weren't allowed to "drive."

All the while we are trying to "control our cars," the Holy Spirit has his hand on the wheel of our lives. Since we are not robots, we can, if we choose, force his hands off of the controls, but then we take responsibility for the failures that follow. For me, it's a real comfort to know he is driving, and in reality I'm just going along for the ride. I like it that way.

One of the ways I resist the Holy Spirit is through my worrying about the road ahead. Maybe you don't have a problem with worry as I do, but often I find myself asking, "What if . . . ?" What if I lose my job? What if I get cancer? What if it snows? What if our child is kidnapped? What if our home burns down? What if the sun burns out? (Some of our worry is just that silly when we look at it in perspective.) Worry, according to one definition, is accepting responsibility for something God never intended us to carry. I've been known to worry about whether it is going to rain on our picnic next week. Since I can't control the weather, why do I worry about it?

The root word of worry means a "divided mind." We go sleepless at night sometimes worrying about the events of the next day. What if we have a flat tire? What if he rejects me? What if I fail? Someone said that 95 percent of the things we worry about never happen. Every other bed in the hospital, it is said, is occupied with a person who is principally there because of stress, anger, bitterness, or worry.

Worry takes a terrible toll on our bodies: heart trouble, high blood pressure, asthma, rheumatism, ulcers, colds, thyroid problems, arthritis, migraine headaches, indigestion, nausea, constipation, colitis, dizziness, fatigue, insomnia, allergies, maybe even paralysis at times. Now obviously, if one of us had some of these problems it could be for other reasons than stress and worry. However, worry can cause problems like this, and if we suffer from such things, it would be good to take an inventory to see just how much worry we are carrying around.

Worry is contagious too. Unless you're married to a worrier, stay away from them—it's just not worth it. They will drag you down with their "What ifs..."

Worry is a sin, because it calls God a liar. Yet it is the most natural human response to struggles and trials. More important than anything I could say about worry is what God has told us:

Who then can ever keep Christ's love from us? When we have trouble or calamity, when we are hunted down or destroyed, is it because he doesn't love us anymore? And if we are hungry, or penniless, or in danger, or threatened with death, has God deserted us? No, for the Scriptures tell us that for his sake we must be ready to face death at every moment of the day—we are like sheep awaiting slaughter; but despite all this, overwhelming victory is ours through Christ who loved us enough to die for us. For I am convinced that nothing can ever separate us from his love. Death can't, and life can't. The angels won't, and all the powers of hell itself cannot keep God's love away. Our fears for today, or worries about tomorrow, or where we are—high above the sky, or in the deepest ocean—nothing will ever be able to separate us from the love of God demonstrated by our Lord Jesus Christ when he died for us (Romans 8:35-39).

It is comforting to know that no matter where we are, nothing can put a wall between us and God's love. God does not want us to look for a way *out* of our problems—he wants us to look for a way *through* them. He'll help us. He promised!

SEVEN

"How to Choke People"

When I was in junior high, notebooks were passed around among the students, with a student's name on each page. They were called "slam books." In them the students would write down anonymously what they thought of each other. Many of the comments were cutting, snide, and hurtful. The only thing I can remember about my name was that someone put down, "He's a good, good guy." I took that to mean I was a "goody-two-shoes." I don't think that's what the person meant, but that's the way I took it. I was sick to my stomach it hurt so bad.

I suppose I thought I *was* a "goody-two-shoes." I didn't go to the dances. I went to movies only when we were in California or somewhere no one would see us. Sometimes after church we would visit some people where we couldn't play ball or read the comics on

Sunday, and we would have to sit around like little angels in our "good clothes."

Dancing or movies or reading comics weren't sins in themselves—I realize that now, as I read the Bible. But I got tired of people with their lists of do's and don'ts, mainly because my list was not the same as their list, and I resented them trying to cram their own taboos down my throat. The church never explained to me why we didn't do certain things. We just didn't do them, and no one knowingly wants to sin. I loved my folks too much to make any waves with dumb questions, so I just stuffed my feelings and went about my business.

But there are good reasons why we as Christians should not do some things the world thinks are fine. For instance, there are many reasons why a person shouldn't smoke. Only a mentally blind person can disregard the mounting evidence of great dangers to the heart and lungs, but millions upon millions of people smoke because they enjoy it, or at least have failed so far to give it up. There's nothing in the Bible that says we shouldn't smoke, but there is the principle that our body is a temple of the Holy Spirit when we become a born-again Christian. That is reason enough for a Christian not to smoke. Since we are earthly representations of Christ, it's really not all that becoming to see Christ going around wheezing, coughing, and blowing smoke all over the place.

Music is another item found on the "lists" of some Christians. Some people give the impression that unless one likes Bach, Chopin, and opera, he is not really a Christian. There is a slight hope for those who like Montovani, or better yet, the golden strings of Ralph Carmichael, but even these musicians are suspect in some circles. Other Christians prefer Bill Gaither music, which has a little more beat. Others enjoy Christian music with a rock sound, while others like all kinds of secular music—country, jazz, even rock and roll.

It seems to me that music is a bit like food. Some people like broccoli (I can't imagine how, but some do), some like asparagus, some banana cream pie, some olives. Taste in music, in my opinion, has no more significance than taste in vegetables. We would not eat toadstools—they would poison our system. We are better off if we don't listen to immoral lyrics, as they poison our system, too. Some churches have fantastic music programs, even orchestras. There are also some people who enjoy singing all five verses of hymn number 576, even though my impression is that the words don't really mean all that much to most people. Some hymns don't seem to have much practical value, at least the way we sing them. Much of the music in our churches seems dead and meaningless to life outside. We are quick to criticize our Jewish brothers for their "tradition" that sometimes becomes more important than the Word itself, but we do the same with music in many of our churches.

The main reason I get concerned about the list of do's and don'ts is the effect it seems to have on non-Christians. They get the impression that we never have any fun, that we are always against anything enjoyable in life. Some Christians do give the impression that they are against everything. They run around with long faces, hoping for the sweet by-and-by, trying to get through this vale of tears with as few scars as possible resulting from contact with the world. A Christian's life should be (and can be) vibrant, fun, exciting, fulfilling, peaceful, and joyful.

Joe Aldrich, in his book, *Lifestyle Evangelism*, talks about developing webs of relationships with our non-Christian friends, so the love of Christ can flow in a natural, non-threatening way from us down those webs into the heart of that precious person for whom Christ died.

We have a number of non-Christian gatherings at our home. I remember one especially. The people arrived, but nothing was happening—no real visiting—a strained feeling of discomfort. Then Barb got the insight that non-Christians usually have their drinks first. So we rushed into the kitchen and prepared the 7-Up and pineapple juice punch everyone loves, and the party took off. Everyone was standing around with this innocent nonalcoholic drink in their hands, visiting, enjoying the moment—comfortable. We were amused with one guy who kept coming back to the punch bowl for more with a quizzical look on his face. I think he was trying to get high on the punch but couldn't make it happen. It was fun to watch.

I was invited once to have lunch with a man with whom I had gone to school. I had witnessed to him on several occasions. He knew I was "straight" because he came from the same kind of home I did with Christian parents, but he had taken another direction with booze, money, fame, flashy cars, rings, clothes, etc. He seemed deliriously happy. Those things *do* bring happiness, for a while. Sin is pleasurable—for a season, as the Bible says. When I arrived, we sat down at the table and he asked me what I wanted to drink. I tried to defer to him, but he insisted, so I ordered my usual Coke. He hesitated for a while and then ordered a Coke, too.

The little waitress nearly split her dress she laughed so hard. "You? A Coke?" You see, this was his favorite restaurant and she knew very well what he drank every day.

I broke in. "Just bring him what he usually has."

And she did—about three martinis. We had a great

time at lunch, except for the momentary crisis a little alcohol can make. He got happier and happier. I did too, because I was loving him right where he was. I'm sure he thought I was going to nail him with some Scripture, or talk about how he was "backsliding" or ask whether or not he was in the Word regularly. But the Lord told me to keep my mouth shut about spiritual things. We talked about business, and the olden days, and the things that were happening in my life. There was not one "spiritual" word spoken, as I remember. But just as he left he looked at me and said, "We've got to get together again soon and talk about some personal things." I knew what he meant. The door was open for our next time together. I really think it was very much a spiritual lunch. He expected condemnation and rejection. I just gave him love. God will provide additional opportunities to get into spiritual things—on his timetable, when he feels the time is right. My job is to be available, and nearby.

There was another time when we were on a trip to a resort hotel and two of our non-Christian friends asked Barb and me out for dinner. We had wanted to get together with these people for a long time, yet never quite got around to it. When we met them in the parking lot to go to the restaurant in the little town nearby, we found that our friend was half-stoned. But we weren't really surprised. We knew he had an alcohol problem. It was his car. He wanted to drive, and rather than giving him a temperance lecture on the evils of demon rum, or insisting that I drive, which would have made him uncomfortable, since this was his "treat," Barb and I just got in the back seat of their little car and away we went. As we often do when we're with another couple, Barb and I began sharing some of the marriage insights we have gained through hard work and failures. In a few minutes, they were also sharing deep things in their relationship, maybe for the first time in their lives, really honest, really open. He weaved a little, but I was sure that God wanted us to honor our friends, and trust him to take care of us. He wasn't out of control—just hampered a touch. I smiled as I noticed that hardly anyone else was on the road. I guess God was out ahead of us, do you suppose?

That evening we had a wonderful time of sharing what the Lord was doing in our lives. They did not become Christians during dinner. In fact, he weaved even more on the way home after a few more drinks. But they both listened. We consider such witnessing as seed-planting. Maybe someone else will have the privilege of "harvesting."

I had breakfast with a young man recently who felt a desire to join a Christian organization, yet had some real doubts about leaving his secular job, and wanted my thoughts. Some of the people he had talked to thought the most "spiritual" thing he could do was join the Christian organization. I wasn't so sure. The more we talked the more obvious it was to both of us what a tremendous mission field he was already on. He told me story after story of people who had come to know the Lord through his witness, and how he was having Bible studies during off hours. He also had a great opportunity to move up quickly in the organization and would soon have great influence on its direction. I haven't seen this person since the day we had breakfast, but at least when he left that morning he was convinced that he could touch many more lives through the secular job than he could with the Christian organization.

I have trouble considering a Christian organization of any kind—even mission groups—as being any more "spiritual" or "important" than working in a machine shop, an advertising agency, a hospital, a department store, or driving a truck. It really doesn't matter where we are. God has a mission field for us, and personally I feel one of the biggest mission fields today is among the hurting, searching, stress-filled people in business.

We are to be ambassadors for Christ wherever we are. That word *ambassador* means "to honor another person, to serve another person, to be concerned about his needs first," just as you and I are to be as we represent Christ as his ambassadors.

I was reading about a young man who lived in a big city condominium. There was a little bit of every kind of sin going on there—immorality, drugs—a real cesspool. He went to his counselor and said that he just had to get out of there. The counselor listened for a while, and then suggested that the young man go back to the condo and look at it as a rich mission field. So he put a note on the bulletin board telling about a Bible study he was going to start in his room on a certain night. He knew no one would show up, but he thought he owed it to the counselor to at least go through the motions. I can't remember the exact timing or numbers, but all of a sudden people actually began to show up, and little by little people's lives were changed through this person's loving witness as he met people right where they were.

One of the things the world can't quite understand is the Christian's willingness to share his faith. After all, religion is a very private thing, we are told. The reason I personally feel a need to share God's Good News of Christ with people is that, first of all, God, in the Bible, asks me to do so. Secondly, I believe hell and eternal punishment are real, and that heaven and eternal bliss are also a reality.

Since I believe what the Bible says about heaven and hell, and the great gulf between the two, I dread the day when I'll be standing on one side of that gulf with my non-Christian friends standing on the other side. I don't fully know all that will happen that day, but I do know that God is just and fair, and that everything he does is right, regardless of what man thinks. Whether or not my non-Christian friends ever receive Christ is not my responsibility. That's God's problem. My responsibility is to love them right where they are and share the Good News of Christ in a natural, non-artificial, non-judgmental way, hoping that something I say or do will help them see that Christ is real.

I was talking the other day to a Christian who is a manager of a small business. Some of the non-Christians on his crew came to him complaining about one of their co-workers who kept bugging them with the Bible. This manager wanted to know whether he should encourage the Christian to keep on in the manner he was or advise him to stop bugging the non-Christians. I don't think the answer is as obvious as it looks at first glance. I advised him to ask the Christian to back off. I don't believe in bugging people to receive Christ. I think our sharing must be a natural part of our lives, like eating and breathing, and we need to use God's opportunities rather than manufactured ones.

On the other hand, no one has ever been led to the Lord through another person's silence. Balance is a principle the Bible stresses over and over in every area of our lives.

Suppose we were traveling down the street, and we saw a beautiful home, and through the big picture window we saw people playing a game having a great time—laughing, joking, and enjoying the moment. We would probably hesitate to knock on the door and break into that atmosphere of fun. But if the roof were on fire, we wouldn't hesitate a minute getting them the message, would we?

We have so many people coming in and out of our lives daily. Effective witnessing usually begins with friendship.

Non-Christians will never accept God's special plan unless someone tells them in a loving, natural, non-threatening way.

I learned a principle in one of the time management seminars I once attended. I was asked to place a star beside that item on my "to-do" list that was the hardest, most unpleasant thing I had to do that day. The next morning I was to do that particular task first, and the rest of my day would be a breeze. It was true. We should witness to the "tough folks" first—our own neighbors—and the rest of the world will be a piece of cake.

The most important thing we can do in witnessing is to get into the Bible and search for truth as we would search for gold or silver. Then when we find those beautiful principles that make living on earth so meaningful, we will have something to share with others. Paul impressed the people he lived with by the honest way he conducted his life. Then they were open to his message about Christ. Unlike Paul, we no longer need the gift of miracles operating in the body of Christ today. Miracles were to authenticate God's representatives who were giving out his Word in the first century. People didn't have a New Testament in Paul's day. It was still being written, so God had to speak through men. The best way to prove the validity of those people who represented him was to give them supernatural powers.

God still performs miracles today, but he no longer needs to authenticate a man. Now he authenticates his Word. The miracles I see the Holy Spirit perform today are seen in the lives of people as anger is controlled, marriages are healed, love replaces hate, and people learn to be servants. Those are all miracles because they are so contrary to our natural way of doing things. One of God's most spectacular miracles today is a changed life.

Joe Aldrich uses the analogy of some department store owners building the most beautiful facility in existence, stocking the shelves with the highest quality goods, hiring the most professional staff available, and then closing all the doors and having the employees sell the goods to each other. People outside the door are peeking in to see if Christianity really works. The only way our non-Christian friends are going to know the truth is for us to open the doors of our lives and let them see first-hand how Christ changes things. The Apostle Paul told of his desire to keep his sermons on the level of the listener. I have heard more pontifical know-it-all preachers than I care to remember. That approach only brings bitter memories to my mind of "dying" in the pew, trying to keep my mind occupied, not having the slightest idea what the speaker was trying to say, counting the bricks in the choir loft.

The Apostle Paul used the analogy of planting to describe the gospel message:

My work was to plant the seed in your hearts, and Apollos' work was to water it, but it was God, not we, who made the garden grow in your hearts. The person who does the planting or watering isn't very important, but God is important because he is the one who makes things grow. Apollos and I are working as a team, with the same aim, though each of us will be rewarded for his own hard work. We are only God's co-workers. You are God's garden, not ours; you are God's building, not ours (1 Corinthians 3:6-9).

We can't all be harvesters. Some of us plant seeds— a word here, a word there, a loving deed here, a touch of concern there. Then some others come along and water the seed to help it sprout. Then the Holy Spirit helps it begin to grow and mature. We are God's helpers—nothing else—his co-workers. The person with whom we share Christ is God's garden, his building. He is the one who brings in the harvest. As we use our special abilities and gifts in seed-planting and watering, God receives the honor and blessing during the harvest.

A former pastor in another state has set up his own ministry. He is helping some people to grow and opening some doors, but I sense that much of the purpose of his ministry is to honor himself rather than God. Only God can judge his heart, but it is terribly easy for someone to begin reading his own press clippings and say to God, "You are really lucky to have me on your team." A true servant is hardly noticed. He is usually in the kitchen or in the basement or out in the yard where no one sees him. When the master is complimented by his guest for the delicious T-bone steak, he says, "Thank you—one of Safeway's finest," but it was really the servant who prepared it. Yet the master is getting all the praise. Our purpose is to honor Christ, not bring honor on ourselves. If our attitudes are right before God, then he will do the honoring at the right place and time. We should not seek honor from men—only from God. Pride is nauseating to God. It's so natural for us to want honor for ourselves and we long for people to say our name or introduce us out of a crowd.

It isn't natural to rejoice when someone else gets the credit for something we have done. The religious leaders of Jesus' day brought attention to themselves as they gave to the poor or prayed or fasted. The Bible says that such glory-seekers have received all the reward they are going to get. The praise we receive from men in response to our good deeds in the name of

Christ is all the reward we will ever get—that's it.
When we do things in secret, or behind the scenes, or
with the attitude that we don't need to be noticed,
then God honors us. Personally I would much rather
be honored by God than by man.

Paul said that "the Kingdom of God is not just talking; it is living by God's power." The more I study the
Bible, the more I am impressed with the number of
times God talks about our behavior, our good deeds—
love, being a servant, forgiving—things we are to do,
not just our talk. Unless our behavior changes after we
receive Christ, we are no different from our non-Christian friends who are looking for a change in our lives
because of our relationship to Christ. If Christianity
doesn't change lives, then the world doesn't need
Christianity.

Some of our greatest, yet toughest, witnessing opportunities happen at home where we live, in front of our
families. Usually one marriage partner comes to know
Christ before the other one, and often it is the wife
first. Part of this could be due to her being more rela-
tionship-oriented than her husband. Generally speaking,
a relationship with God through Christ, or relationships
in the body of believers, would be more appealing to a
woman than a man. A man often needs to see the log-
ic, the facts, and the numbers all have to make sense.
Personally, I believe the maintenance of the marriage
relationship when only one partner is a Christian falls
almost completely on the shoulders of the one who
knows the power of the Holy Spirit living within. Some
men are terribly threatened by their wives' involvement
in the church. Sometimes the woman does not use wisdom with respect to her church activities. She is usually so excited about her new life that she wants to
spend every waking moment at the church or with her
new Christian friends. We can all understand, however,
that her husband feels completely left out. She doesn't

have as much time for his needs as she did before, and naturally he blames the church for stealing his wife's affections.

I told one wife that the most spiritual thing she could do on a particular Sunday morning was to go camping with her husband rather than coming to church. She began to do that, and it wasn't long before he was making sure she was in church on those weekends when they weren't camping. He was beginning to be won over through her soft, gentle, and cooperative spirit. The reason we are left here on earth is because God has someone else with whom he wants us to share the wonderful news of Christ. Our purpose for being here is not just to do advertising, or turn out washing machine parts, or sell soup, or be a homemaker, or run a bulldozer. Our greater purpose is to live Christ in front of the people in our lives so that they will want to know more about why we are different.

It is a privilege to be one of Christ's ambassadors, representing him to the people around us. What we do, how we live, our attitude, our priorities, all reflect on Jesus Christ. Some of the people in our lives wouldn't be caught dead in a church or listening to the local Christian radio station, or watching Billy Graham on TV. Their only exposure to the Good News might be what we live before them, and the words we share with them. We are ambassadors for Christ—what an honor! The Apostle Paul wrote:

We try to live in such a way that no one will ever be offended or kept back from finding the Lord by the way we act, so that no one can find fault with us and blame it on the Lord. In fact, in everything we do we try to show that we are true ministers of God. We patiently endure suffering and hardship and trouble of every kind (2 Corinthians 6:3, 4).

If our lives are full of bitterness, anger, lust, dishonesty, laziness, and lying, and the people around us know that we are Christians, we could easily hinder them from thinking that receiving Christ would make any difference in their lives. The more I read the Bible, the more I notice the thread running through it—good works, deeds of kindness, obedience, good behavior—doing! Our life-style shouts to the housetops who we really are. When we endure hardship, suffering, and trouble, confident that God has a reason and purpose for our lives, people can't help but notice the supernatural strength within us. Then they really have no choice but to assume that our Christianity has something to do with it.

EIGHT
66 Life in the Pits 99

I had been working so hard at the office that I was getting bitter and resentful. I have to keep the business healthy in order to pay for the various ministries God has given us. I have chosen to keep the staff small and try to do a great deal of the client contact personally. All I really have to sell is me, and I want to serve my customers so well that they won't even consider looking for another agency. I do a lot of things free to show them I can give as well as receive in business.

Staying so close to the business, however, means that I have to be involved in much more detail than I might if I were working for someone else. When my client wants to know why we're paying a premium for drive time in Prosser when the city is only two miles wide, I want to be able to give him an instant answer as often as possible. I hate to say, "I'll check on it and get back." Obviously there are times when I have to do this, since I'm only human. But I like to keep those times to a minimum by trying to be very knowledge-able about my business.

I often have to do a delicate balancing act, because I have so many ministry-type things I want to do. This balancing of priorities may be my toughest job.

Once in a while, at one of my regular morning ses-sions, I'll suggest to the Lord that he find me a nice little gold mine close to the house, or maybe in the basement, where I could go and chip off what I need for that month to live, and then spend my time coun-seling, ministering, and loving my Christian and non-Christian friends full time. The Lord thinks about this for a few seconds and then reminds me that some of the people I want to relate to wouldn't give me the time of day if they didn't know I experienced the same pressures they did—profit and loss statements, employ-ee turnover, time pressures, pension plans, overhead growth, etc.

So I return to the business at hand, and once again put my nose into the day-to-day details. Meanwhile I squeeze in early breakfasts, long lunches, and late phone conversations with the people I feel God has asked me to love for him. As the problems and chal-lenges of the business begin to mount and more and more people come into my life to love for Christ, the time pressures become almost unbearable so that I be-gin to resent the next person who needs just a few minutes of my time. Or someone needs a "simple" slide presentation for his church, or some financial advice, or employment counseling, or help to find God's will for his life in some area. I know that God doesn't want me to be bitter and resentful, so I start cutting back on those things I find myself involved in—good things—but not maybe the best things.

One of the comforting thoughts, as I am buried up

to my eyes in projects, is to reflect on what Christ said at the end of his ministry. He said his job was "finished." Yet there were lepers, blind people, and other hurting folks all around him. What this suggests to me is that I should be very careful with my priorities so that I am working on the most important thing at any given moment. So if there are some projects I don't get done, that's really God's problem. He will either impress on me to find the time to get them done or give someone else the blessing. When I get so tied up in knots, I really don't do a good job at anything.

There are many books on the subject of anger. I'll not try to duplicate them, but I do want to share some insights from my own experience on this emotion, which plagues me from time to time.

A few months ago, as my anger, frustration, and bitterness were increasing daily because of time pressures, there came a Saturday when I had no immediate deadlines. I had only one person coming over for counseling. It was almost a free day and I was relishing the thought of puttering around my workshop or playing some tennis. Maybe I would read a book, or do some of the other 119 projects I wanted to do.

That day the sun came out, brighter than usual for Seattle. After breakfast, my sweet wife approached me with some projects to do. We had invited a group of tennis players and swimmers over for the next day. I was to bring up the tables, put chlorine in the pool, clean the filter, lay out the pickle-ball court, prepare the barbecue, clean off my desks, pick up junk in the basement, sweep out the garage, sort my books into piles, and other stuff on her list. Both Barb and I read before we go to sleep at night, so there is always a big pile of books by our bed. She often reminds me that our insurance policy should have a special clause in it that says we are covered if she ever falls over my books when she is making the bed. Sorting books into piles on Saturday is something I can handle. No problem.

Then Barb threw in the ringer. She also wanted the pie cherries picked from a tree we have in our backyard. For the entire time we have lived in this home, the squirrels have eaten every cherry before we have had a chance to get out to pick them. They even crawl along the branches upside down to get the last ones.

But this year, the little monsters were asleep or something, or on vacation. Who knows? Anyway, the tree was loaded with cherries, and not a squirrel in sight. There is something chemical between a woman and a tree, because Barb has this thing about fruit being picked when it is ripe. As far as I am concerned, those cherries were to feed God's furry little friends and we were meant to buy what we need at the Safeway store. There's a Scripture on this subject, which escapes me for the moment.

Anyway, there they were—luscious, red, fat, ripe, juicy cherries, crying out to Barb, "Pick us!"

Where are you, you dumb squirrels? Why haven't you done your job this year?

Now I realize some of you "cherry pickers" can't relate to what I'm feeling. You want them, and so does Barb, to put them in pies that we can't eat anyway because we're too fat. I couldn't believe I was being asked to sacrifice my very good Saturday for something like this! Anyway, I got the dumb ladder, the stupid bucket on a wire to hang on my belt, and climbed this ridiculous tree to pick some idiotic fruit, which seemed to be splitting its seams laughing at me. From my standpoint, it was stupid for me to use the time for which I had longed and prayed—just a little extra free time from the pressures of work and ministries —to do what I wanted to do for once—not what I *had* to do. Here I am picking dumb things that Barb could buy at

Safeway for 39 cents a pound, and as far as stewardship is concerned, I could sit at my typewriter and
make many times that amount in the same period of
time. So it all just didn't make sense.

I can also hear all of you fruit pickers taking me to
task for wanting to waste fruit. It wasn't wasted. The
squirrels ate it. It was fantastic nutrition for them. We
were taking care of God's creatures. God does not
want us to be cruel to his animals, picking off their
very life blood from trees.

I was so angry I couldn't believe it. I can't remember
when I've been so upset over such a minor thing. It
ruined my entire day and part of the next one, too. I
could hardly speak to anyone, especially Barb. I hated
everything that came into my path.

And then to top it off, Barb asked me to wash the
umbrella over the picnic table. I doubt whether the
people coming over would even notice we had an umbrella, let alone whether or not it was dusty (OK,
dirty). Who cares? Barb does, and that does make a
difference.

So I helped clean the umbrella after I got done picking the stupid cherries. I rigged up the power nozzle
that my daughter, Bev, gave me for my birthday. I
aimed the nozzle at the umbrella only to find out that
it was in danger of being torn to shreds by the power
of the stream, so we had to scrub it by hand.

Then I had to clean the filter on the pool. It had mi-
croscopic holes in the little screen, which seemed to
get plugged when extra large atoms went through.
Every three minutes I had to clean it out or it wouldn't
work properly. All right, maybe not quite *that* often.

I had tried to convince Barb that cleaning the filter
was "way over my head" complicated. Earlier in my
life I would put the plastic things in the wrong place in
the dishwasher, or mess up the kids changing diapers
until Barb would say, "Let me do it." Then I would go

read or something. This time the jig was up. She *taught* me to clean the filter, and it was too simple to make her think I didn't understand. You have to travel a half mile (at least twenty feet) to get to the controls that turn off the water so you can take off the filter, clean the stupid thing, put it back together, hike back the three miles to turn the water on again, come back the four miles to find that the fittings weren't tight enough, stumble back to turn the water off again, back to adjust the fittings, back to the controls. My whole life was passing before my eyes. The world was dying from starvation, and what am I doing about it? Picking cherries, scrubbing umbrellas, and cleaning filters. I wondered how long God was going to stand for this type of stewardship on my part.

That Saturday brought a fitting end to a whole week of anger and frustration. I won't bore you with all the details, but it was terrible. I had so many expectations and so little fulfillment! The typewriter broke down, two of my employees had traffic accidents, the copy machine broke down, I couldn't find essential films and tapes, and Saturday was just the last straw.

And then I found out what was the matter. I had agreed to speak at our church on Sunday evening and the topic I had chosen months ago was "Anger." The Lord was making me live what I was going to teach about. He was intending to speak through my experiences to make them real to the people who would hear. They could only relate to me if they felt I knew what I was talking about and had lived it.

Our assistant pastor had noted the growth of the Sunday morning class Barb and I teach. I told him it was God who was bringing the people, but one of the things we had found was that when Barb and I are real, transparent, and open about our past and present failures and struggles, people seem to relate to us and

Amen!

learn more than if we just teach in the third person and sound as if we have solved everything.

The assistant pastor told me his training in seminary had emphasized that pastors and teachers were always to keep a little distance between the pulpit and pew, and not to be too real—just the opposite of what Scripture teaches, as far as I could see. I told him that was the main reason why it took me thirty-eight years to get to the point—that Christ could be real in my life.

Christ didn't spend much time behind a pulpit. He was in the street surrounded by the hurting people who could relate to his love and care. We have to be real, and that includes admitting our anger and our struggles. People and situations don't cause our anger—they just reveal it! We have the anger inside us. People and situations are just the occasion for it to come out. When I get on the freeway or city streets, people conspire to impede my way. Some jerk up ahead wants to turn left, and there are 405 cars and trucks waiting behind him, including me. So what if that's his driveway? The least he could do is come home at a decent hour, or turn around, come back on the other side of the street and turn right with no time-wasting left turns to irritate people and get them angry.

Are you getting the picture? People are out to get me. I go into the bank and see four lines, three of which have fifty-eight people waiting. The other line has only two people, an innocent looking lady and a young boy. I opt for that line, and find out why the other people are in the other lines. The lady is trying to cash a fifty-year-old Social Security check she found in a drawer and it takes a series of calls to the bank headquarters in Oakland to get the matter straightened out. The young man is bringing in his penny collection, which requires five hours to count, and by now the fifty-eight other people in the other lines have gone through and now there are eighty-two people in each line, one of which I now join.

When I began my study on anger, I first went to the concordance to see if anger was ever mentioned in the Bible. I found three entire columns of single-spaced Scripture references relating to anger, and much of it was talking about God's anger:

But Moses pleaded, "O Lord, I'm just not a good speaker. I never have been, and I'm not now, even after you have spoken to me, for I have a speech impediment." "Who makes mouths?" Jehovah asked him. "Isn't it I, the Lord? Who makes a man so that he can speak or not speak, see or not see, hear or not hear? Now go ahead and do as I tell you, for I will help you to speak well, and I will tell you what to say." But Moses said, "Lord, please! Send someone else." Then the Lord became angry (Exodus 4:10-14).

I can just feel God's anger in this passage. He had given Moses all the gifts and talents he needed to do God's work, but he still had no self-confidence and wanted God to "send someone else." God got angry with Moses, and I'm afraid he gets angry with me, too, as I forget that he is in control, not me.

Jesus on occasion was angry:

While in Capernaum Jesus went over to the synagogue again, and noticed a man there with a deformed hand. Since it was the Sabbath, Jesus' enemies watched him closely. Would he heal the man's hand? If he did, they planned to arrest him! Jesus asked the man to come and stand in front of the congregation. Then turning to his enemies, he asked, "Is it all right to do kind deeds on Sabbath days? Or is

*this a day for doing harm? Is it a day to save lives
or to destroy them?" But they wouldn't answer him.
Looking around at them angrily, for he was deeply
disturbed by their indifference to human need, he
said to the man, "Reach out your hand." He did, and
instantly his hand was healed!* (Mark 3:1-5).

I get the impression from this last Scripture and others that the religious leaders of the day were the ones
who were most often on the receiving end of Christ's
anger. But unlike Christ's anger, mine is not righteous
as I zero in on the present-day Pharisees. Paul said
that we judge in others those weaknesses we find in
ourselves. I, too, tend to be critical, intolerant, and unloving, finding it easy to hold grudges.

There is no way Jesus Christ, when he cleared out
the temple, could turn over those tables without anger
boiling inside him as he saw his Father's house being
used as a marketplace. There is one big difference between Jesus and me, of course, and that is that he did
not sin with his anger, and I do. But it helps me a
great deal to know that he experienced the same feelings I have. It makes him more real, easier for me to
believe as one who understands me when I get angry.
He experienced all of my temptations and pressures
and did not sin.

Just what is anger, this frustration, this rage that
sometimes tears us apart and makes us explode, hurting the ones we love? Sometimes it surprises us as we
wonder where in the world it comes from. Anger is an
emotion caused by the frustration of our goals and desires. It can be brought on by people, situations, or
things.

Some of the things that cause my anger you may not
understand, because you have other things in your life
which drive you batty. For instance, I recently tried to
get some masking tape off our cement driveway, which

had been placed there to mark out a playing court for a game with a group of people we had over for a visit. The sun and the cars had mashed the tape into the crevices of the cement, and now I had to take it up in bitty pieces, and I didn't want to take the time to deal with little tiny pieces of tape. I wanted it to come up in one large strip so I could spend thirty seconds at the most getting rid of it, and then get on with the important things in life such as the football game I was missing.

I get angry when I can't find something—a tool or piece of sports equipment that I know was right here. I can see it in my mind. It was there just a minute ago. Someone must have moved it. Now most of the time (Barb would say "a few times," but what does she know?) someone does take it, probably to see me squirm. Once in a great while—I remember a time on May 17, 1956, and once on December 14, 1964—that it was I who mislaid it and forgot where I had placed it last. Those are the only two times I can remember when it was my fault. Most of the time, Satan or one of the members of my family moves whatever it is I'm looking for, and it drives me out of my mind.

We used to have what I called "the Bermuda Triangle," our dining room table. Now, let me ask you, what is a dining room table for? All together now with our answer, "To leave things on." Right? Right. To leave things on. You can eat on it, too, but it is placed near the front door purposely so you can leave stuff on it when you come home from work or play. For some reason, Barb thinks it should never have anything on it—ever! When the kids or I would put something down on the table, it would disappear, never to be seen again, just like the ships and planes in the real Bermuda Triangle. Poof! Not even any ashes. I used to get angry at not being able to find something I had left there. Now I have victory over that. We moved, and our present dining room table is three miles from the front door, so now I use the entryway table, but so far the strange force has not discovered that particular spot.

Anger is no stranger to me. I experience it often, but the Lord is working on that part of me, helping me fail less often as I study what causes my anger.

When you think about it, I guess we were born into the world angry. After spending nine beautiful months in that warm nest with every one of our needs being met, all of a sudden we experienced cold air, a slap on the bottom, and a bunch of strangers around. But soon we found comfort at our mother's breast, feeling her warmth once again, and if we stayed dry and were fed regularly and cuddled a lot, we felt pretty good about life. But try to frustrate one of our goals and look out!

In the book *Facing Anger* by Norman Rohrer and Philip Sutherland (Augsburg, 1981), I learned there are several basic reasons for anger. The first one is the desire to feel powerful. We feel weak if our behavior is determined by other people, so we become angry in order to restore our sense of power. The person who feels powerful doesn't need anger. The person who doesn't worry about tomorrow has power, but the worrier feels weak because he doesn't know what tomorrow will bring. There are all kinds of power struggles—between husband and wife, parent and child, brothers and sisters, employees and bosses. I can't think of a relationship where there might not be a struggle for power.

Another thing that makes some of us angry is having too many things to do in too little time. I have always prided myself in getting a lot done, even though it makes me angry at times when I get into a time squeeze. I even did six things at once fairly recently. I was dubbing a tape, working on a slide presentation, putting a record on a cassette, filling the fountain, flushing the car radiator, and running some copies on my little copy machine. After I finished that record-breaking accomplishment, I rushed upstairs to share this triumph with Barb, but guess what? She wasn't the least bit impressed.

I had read the book *Type A Behavior and Your Heart* (Friedman and Rosenman, Knopf, 1974), which seemed to indicate that people who were on the go, made impossible deadlines for themselves, hated red lights, had lots of stress, and couldn't relax, were more prone to heart attacks than Type B people, who relaxed and took things a little more easily, who didn't mind traffic signals, and did only what they could do in the time allowed, doing one thing at a time. Barb reminded me that I wasn't supposed to do more. I was supposed to do less.

I really get angry when I'm late, which is often caused by trying to do too much at the last minute, or having too many people demanding my time.

Anger is not actually produced by a situation so much as it is our interpretation of the situation. For instance, Barb feels that red lights are ordained by God to bring order into our lives. I feel red lights are direct tools of Satan to disrupt my schedule.

There's a red light on a street by our home that I've asked the city to remove. It is in a lonely part of the neighborhood, protecting a street that is seldom used. In fact, only twice in recorded history has anyone come from the other direction. Once on May 14, 1933, Mazie Rathknocker lost her way and came up there and the other time was August 23, 1962, when Henry Radburner took the wrong turn. Other than those two instances, no one has ever used that red light. And it irritates me to have to stop when no one ever comes the other way.

Other things make us angry because of our loss of

power, such as death. Many times people feel angry when a person close to them has died, even becoming angry at the dead person himself. Or maybe someone loses his house in a flood, or a fire burns it to the ground, or a burglar cleans out the house, or a car accident leaves family members hospitalized. We feel absolutely helpless in such situations. We have no power over the event, which makes us angry.

Another cause of anger is our desire to be self-sufficient. The young child wants to put on his or her own socks. The teenager wants to fix the car. The young wife struggles to sew a dress. There's nothing wrong with trying to do these things, but when we fail at our task, we become angry and frustrated. We want to be in control and sometimes this causes us not to see doctors, seek counsel, weep, or ask someone for financial help. We want to do it ourselves, and when we lose control, we get angry.

As a general rule, I would much rather go to a restaurant than to someone's home. In someone's home, I'm not in control as far as the food they serve is concerned. The problem with going to someone's home is that they want to put on the dog, so they have cream of broccolisoufflevichyssoise or something just as elegant. Cooked vegetables and I have never gotten along. In fact, I don't think it is scriptural to eat them. Somewhere there is a verse in Second Sampson that says (from one translation), "Cursed is the cook who boileth the weed in its own juice and crammeth it down the throat of the brethren." I think if God had wanted us to eat cooked vegetables he would have grown them already cooked.

I loved one of the Christian education directors we had at church, but he was a little on the "systems and programs" side of things. During the first couple of years we worked together, he would take me out to

lunch, admit that it appeared that our class was growing and healthy, but he had this great stuff from one of
the Christian publishing houses he thought I should be
teaching. Each time I explained to him that I could
only teach those things that I have lived, and would
not necessarily be living page 294 just because it came
after page 293 in the material.

My point is that I have lived struggling with anger,
so God brings into my life people who need what I've
learned. Trying to be self-sufficient hits the home, too,
as fathers and husbands try to be in control of their
wives and kids. It's so hard for a man to say, "I'm sorry," or "Please forgive me." We want to hide the problem under the rug, bluster around until we get the
upper hand, never admitting our failures and faults.
The family then sees us as insensitive and uncaring.

We wound each other's spirits with the things we do
and say. For instance, when I first found out about
Type A and B persons, I used to say to people that
Barb wasn't a B—she was a D minus (because it was
hard for her to keep up with me). Pow! It was like a
big rock right into her spirit. Teasing is a form of anger and does much to close a person's spirit to us.
When the spirit closes, so do the emotions, as does
our physical relationship as man and wife.

It is absolutely mind-boggling what our wives do
sometimes. For instance, there have been times when
Barb and I would have a conflict and she would go to
the bedroom to cry. I would cautiously make my way
up there after steeling my courage and would be greeted with "Go away." So in my logical brain, being used
to dealing with facts and doing what people say, I
would go away. But that is not what she really needed.
She really wanted me to "Come here, hold me in your
arms," but she said, "Go away."

Now that's tough to explain to a man, but it's true

and it is up to the husband to live with his wife in understanding so he can do the right thing, which is not always (to him) the logical thing.

To such a man I suggest he take his wife out to a quiet restaurant or some place private and talk. I had closed Barb's spirit over the years, in numerous ways, making her my best joke when I taught, losing money on six occasions when I did not take her counsel, plus a whole bunch of other things that had offended her over the years.

I asked Barb's forgiveness for each of the things I could remember that I knew had hurt her. Talk about a teary evening! I pretty much remembered all the times I'd offended Barb, but after you have covered all the things you can remember, you might ask your wife if there are other things you have forgotten. Chances are she will say something like, "Remember that time at my folks when you got so angry?" So, take care of that too. When you open her spirit, then she opens to you emotionally and physically at the same rate. This is not a once-for-all thing. Do it as often as you need to keep short accounts of the hurts. Wives can open husbands' spirits, too, as can parents for kids and employees for bosses. Any relationship can be healed with this process.

Another cause of anger is wanting to feel important, to be first in line, president of the club, captain of the team, to win at everything we try. Some of that drive can stem from childhood where we have been told by someone in our lives that we would "never amount to anything."

I had lunch once with a young man who was a workaholic, a driven man. I found out that he was still trying to prove his worth to his father, who had been dead for ten years.

Another cause of anger is our striving for perfection.

[handwritten margin notes: because we are constantly told we don't measure up by those of us more "spiritual"... only how we measure...]

The straight A student gets all bent out of shape when she gets a B, the concert pianist hits a wrong note, the mechanic strips a thread, the football player fumbles the ball, the baseball player strikes out. Many people feel they have to be perfect to be accepted. When they don't do a spectacular job, they feel like a failure and get angry. Sometimes we reach for unrealistic expectations, goals for which we do not have the ability, time, patience, or resources to reach.

We also expect perfection from our kids and get angry when we don't get it. People who see themselves as perfect have a hard time accepting criticism. It makes them angry to learn about their imperfections.

I sometimes give the assignment in our Sunday morning class: "Go out and destroy an enemy this week." Obviously you have to know the context. I mean that by loving an enemy, he ceases to be an enemy. Therefore, you have "destroyed" him or her as an enemy. In fact, many times you become friends, believe it or not.

One time a woman in the class, after hearing the assignment, baked three pies, because she was having trouble with three different neighborhood families. She took the pies to the neighbors, asking them to forgive her unloving attitude. And do you know? She healed those relationships! I don't know all the details, but I'm pretty sure that the neighbors were the ones mostly to blame for the ill feelings, but because she was obedient, God honored her for it.

It's natural for us to want the other person to come to us and ask forgiveness first, especially when he is wrong. But that is the point. Even if we are only 10 percent wrong, we should take care of our part of the problem. And then be careful not to say, "If I have offended you, please forgive me." Actually what you are saying is *if*, but we must leave out the *if* and ask his forgiveness. Let God worry about his reaction and whether he ever takes care of his part. Most of the time the other person will say, "Sure, but would you forgive me, too?" And there is instant healing.

However, you may run into someone who responds, "It's about time you asked my forgiveness. You really were a jerk, and still are."

Now, do the rules change? Do you bust him in the nose? No. That's God's problem.

My son, Tim, was having some problems with a foreman, and he asked the man's forgiveness for his bad attitude or whatever it was that offended him. The man responded harshly, "Don't you ever do that again! That's a sign of weakness." But you know, I'm told that Tim was one of his favorites after that, and their conflict was resolved. Tim was mostly in the right, but he did it God's way and God honored him for it.

Another young woman came up after the "destroy an enemy" assignment and said the only person with whom she didn't get along was a sister, but I didn't mean sisters, did I? I pointed out that sisters are some of the most important enemies we can destroy, and even if her sister was in Texas, she could use the telephone. The sister's son answered the phone, and there was a bad connection—the perfect reason for her to hang up. There *was* someone who didn't want the call to go through—Satan. Anyway, the sister finally came to the phone. I don't know all the details, but the bottom line after Sandy asked her sister's forgiveness was the response, "What in the world is going on up there?" When she saw Sandy was serious, the relationship was restored as a result of Sandy's obedience.

Meekness is really the key to overcoming anger—accepting everything that comes into our lives as being designed or allowed by God. He knows all about it, and he never makes mistakes. We need to be realistic about our lives and accept the truth of our limits.

We should make an inventory of all the things that

cause us to become angry and then present the list to God, asking him to help us control the anger so other people in our lives will see that we have supernatural strength to handle our anger. That way, we can be of value to others who might struggle with this same problem, and they can see that we have the answer.

NINE

"The Garbage Man Never Came"

My first memory of school was a snowy day in kindergarten when I walked into the closed-in porch of an annex where we had our classes. I saw all the "big" boys' and girls' snow boots and wet coats, all hung up on hooks, dripping on the floor. I remember wondering if I would ever be that big. They seemed so confident and important, those first-graders! I saw them on the playground and it was awesome to see how mature they were. The next thing I remember is graduating from kindergarten and going in to first grade.

I cried a lot in the first grade, as I remember, or at least was on the verge of tears much of the time. I've always had a sensitive spirit and even now things easily move me to tears. I never watch animal movies. Barb wants me to watch the *Black Stallion* movie we have on tape. No way! I'm sure a cruel owner or a tragedy in the horse's life will make me cry, and I feel weak when I cry.

I also don't like relationship movies or TV shows where Grandpa dies, or the husband and father goes off to war, or the little child is run over, or the high school girl is jilted, or the dog gets crippled, or the mother gets hurt in a car accident. Just give me *F Troop*, *McHale's Navy*, and *The Roadrunner*. The only tears I have from those programs are because I laugh so hard.

One of my pals in fourth grade, Chuck Williams, stuck a pencil on the chair just as I sat down and the lead went into my flesh and broke off. The teacher had to take me into the hall closet and pick it out with a needle. How mortifying! I remember the big boys talked and laughed about things in the bathroom that didn't make much sense, but it sounded naughty, so I laughed too, wanting to be part of the group.

I loved soccer and could hardly wait for soccer season. One day we would put away our baseball bats and out would come the soccer balls. No bells were rung. It was not on anyone's calendar, as far as I know. We just knew that baseball was over and soccer was in. You would have been a nerd to continue playing baseball then, and nobody wanted to be a nerd!

Then there was the time when I spilled hot chocolate from my thermos in the lunchroom and Rosemary Bowe, one of the big sixth graders, helped me clean it up. She was so nice and helpful, and didn't bawl me out. I was so grateful! She later married Robert Stack, the movie star.

Then came the big day when I went to junior high for the first time. What else is there to learn? How big can you get? What other heights could one possibly attain? Imagine—junior high!

My first shock came when I went into the lunchroom with my brown bag and saw teachers right in the same room with us, and they were eating! I couldn't believe it. Teachers were supposed to be in the classroom all the time—days, nights, holidays! They were just there. They didn't have families or eat or drive cars or laugh at jokes. And for sure, they didn't smoke. All of a sudden I was seeing teachers laugh, eat out of brown bags, have fun, right there in front of everyone. What a shock! They were almost like people.

I enjoyed the shop classes the most—metal, wood, and electric shop. I'm still using some of the skills I learned there. I also began to notice that those other people were actually girls. They had long hair and wore dresses, so it wasn't too hard to figure out which were boys and which were girls.

School was easy for me. I learned to give the teachers back what they wanted, whether I understood it or not. And that seemed to satisfy the system. I remember most of my book reports were on chapter 7: "The part I liked best was in chapter 7 where Todd Forthright lost his way on the trail and the wolf...." I figured that if the teacher thought I got all the way to chapter 7, I must have finished the book. I was too smart to read the first or last chapter. Chapter 7 seemed just about right and that was the only chapter I ever read.

My dad used to take me to grade school in his Model A Ford. The school was about a mile away from home. If I sat very still and didn't say anything, he would drive past the school and take me to his work. Pretty soon he would wake up to the fact that I was still in the car and he would backtrack to the school and let me off. I never remember a time that he was anything but amused. I look back at that with wonderment because I probably would have been bent out of shape with anger if one of my kids had done that to me, since I'm always in such a hurry to get somewhere.

When my son, Tim, was born I took his birth in

stride. Prior to that time, babies were pretty much to be left to the care of their mothers who seem to understand them. Fathers can't seem to relate to spitting up, messy diapers, cries in the night. God never designed a man to take that type of stress, so mothers should protect their husbands from this until the babies are six months old. Once they start smiling, cooing, and responding, then they are fun.

I failed Tim repeatedly as he was growing up by not allowing him to be little the way my parents had allowed me to be little. I always considered him more "grown up" than he really was. Tim also had a sensitive spirit, just like mine, that I didn't recognize. We would play the card game "Old Maid," and if he got the Old Maid, tears would begin gathering in his eyes. Bev, who had a better self-image, would try to get the Old Maid from him so he would feel better.

About the seventh grade or so, Tim began removing himself from family activities. We didn't realize at the time that part of it was due to his beginning to smoke at a young age and he had to hide it. I really violated the biblical principles of understanding my family. I didn't invest the time to know how Tim was put together.

Tim went through some tough years as a teenager. He began treating his mom terribly and I took up the offense for Barb and cut off any meaningful relationship with Tim. In hindsight, what I should have done was express my sadness and displeasure at how he was treating his mom, but maintain an open relationship with him. I should not have based my love on his performance. I really failed him and have asked his forgiveness for my stupidity and ignorance. I had no idea how to discipline, so I just punished.

I remember an experience we had with the garbage. Growing up on a farm, I had lots of work to do—feed the chickens, cows, horses, pigs, clean out the barn, water the garden, gather the eggs, and pick the apples. There was no time for "I don't feel like it." I just did the chores because that was why I was there, and besides, the cows and chickens—bunch of tattletales—would complain loudly if I didn't get their feed on time. Since I had to work so hard when I was young, I thought, of course, that Tim should do the same. Only we were city slickers now, and there wasn't all that much for city kids to do. There *was* the garbage, however, so that seemed to be a good place to begin responsibility training.

My dad always emptied the garbage, and I had done it while the kids were small. But now that Tim was an "adult" in first grade, he should show some spunk. So Tim was assigned the garbage. I would casually mention, "Tim, the garbage is getting a little full. Would you please empty it after school?"

School came and went. "Tim, would you empty the garbage before dinner, please?"

Dinner came and went. "Tim, before you go to bed, would you please take out the garbage."

Bedtime came and went. "Tim, before you leave for school, [louder now] would you *please* take out the garbage?"

School came and went. "TIM, IF YOU DON'T GET THE DUMB GARBAGE EMPTIED BEFORE DINNER, I'LL HAVE YOUR HIDE!"

Dinner came, and since I didn't know what "having his hide" really meant, and since the garbage was smelling a bit by this time, I took out the garbage and became more frustrated and bitter as the battle started all over again.

It was my impression that he never took out the garbage except one time when he did it on his own without our asking. I failed him once again by not falling all over him with grateful praise, having a neighborhood celebration, bronzing the garbage can. Instead, I simply said to myself, "It's about time he took a little responsibility around here," and my face, of course, showed my thoughts and that ruined the whole thing. What I should have done was to make him feel really important, and then he would have taken it out on his own, again and again.

(As Tim was proofreading this book for me, he made the comment that he took out the garbage lots of times, when his mom asked. But with me it was a power struggle, he said.)

Another way I failed Tim was not to allow him to have feelings, the same conflict I had with Barb. I hate conflict. When someone raises his voice or expresses negative feelings, I either want him to be quiet or I want to walk away. I hate confrontation with every fiber of my being. Yet over the years that has been the very thing that has helped me grow as a person. When Tim would express anger, I would tell him to be quiet, to go to his room, or to quit talking to his mother like that. There was no effort on my part to find out what was bugging him—lack of attention, something wrong at school or with the kids in the neighborhood, the pressures of growing up. I could never quite fight my way through my angry feelings to get to the root of the matter.

When it was Tim's turn to do the dinner dishes, he would sometimes still be doing them at ten o'clock at night. I don't know how he passed the time, but he did. Our whole evening was consumed with keeping him on the job. When the child constantly wins the power struggle, he loses respect for authority, which molds thinking patterns for adult life. We have a whole generation of people out there running around with no respect for authority. They cross the streets wherever they want, go through red lights, boo the politicians introduced at ball games, shake their fist at the police, grow pot in their gardens. Many of these attitudes begin at home.

Sometimes we parents simply do not invest the time it takes to rear our children properly. Believe it or not, kids want rules, and even though they may fight them, they really desire having standards to live by. When we don't care enough to correct our children, they get the message that they are not important enough in our lives for us to take the time to be involved in their world.

We should have as few rules in our families as possible, and those few that are necessary should be strictly enforced. We should draw a line and make sure the child knows that if he steps over the line, he will get his toe smashed. Almost all children will test it and put their toe over the line. At that point, many parents simply draw another line, and the child will test that one, and then the parent moves the line again and the child tests it again.

Kids are not dumb. They don't like to get their toes smashed any more than the parents like to smash them. It's just that after they have determined that you mean what you say, the power struggle will be over for that particular rule.

We explained the concept to some friends of ours with regard to their teenage girl who wanted to go to a dance. The parents felt it would be best if she stayed home. She cried and cried for hours, but they didn't give in. Some time later, they found a note from one of the girl's younger sisters, written back and forth in school with a friend. The note said, "Ask your mom if you can go to the dance." The reply was, "My folks won't let me." The friend wrote back, "Just ask ask ask ask ask." The girl's reply was, "My sister cried for three hours and it didn't do a bit of good."

Parents are their own worst enemies when they give

in too soon to the power struggle. It is best for everyone concerned if they remain firm, no matter how hot it gets. I tended to overlook problems just because I didn't want the hassle. Then after three or four problems in a row, I erupted in anger that was much more explosive than the offense deserved.

Solomon wrote, "Discipline your son in his early years while there is hope. If you don't you will ruin his life" (Proverbs 19:18). In another place he wrote, "Don't fail to correct your children; discipline won't hurt them! They won't die if you use a stick on them! Punishment will keep them out of hell" (Proverbs 23:13, 14).

During the "Spock" era, when the kids were supposed to do their own thing with little or no parental interference, this Scripture was ignored by non-Christians and by some Christians as well. Our newspapers today are full of stories of murders and violence, the products of people insisting on having their own way— no rules, with the philosophy, "No limits," or "If it feels good, do it."

I don't know what child psychologists say about using a stick, but I think it's probably a good idea. It's the same principle used in training dogs. If you use your hand for spanking, then they become hand-shy when you reach down to just pet them. They think they are going to get another swat. When you use a neutral object such as a small stick or wooden spoon or a newspaper, the child like the dog will attach the hurt to the object, and not to you.

We had a wooden paddle I made with Tim's name on one side and Bev's on the other. The "Tim" side was worn a little more than the "Bev" side because Bev, being the second child, observed the things Tim did to get himself in trouble and avoided them. I remember the time we heard Bev crying and fussing in the bedroom, and as usual we called out, "Tim, stop hitting your sister." But it continued, so we dropped what we were doing and went to the bedroom and found Bev pounding her fists into Tim, yelling at the top of her voice.

We probably punished Tim in error many times. I really don't know how he made it. Yet, today he looks back on his upbringing with understanding rather than bitterness. In fact, I got a note from him recently, reminding me once again that he felt I did what I thought best in raising him.

The problem was one of trust. He would try to talk his way out of something and we would find out later he had fibbed to us. Then we would trust him a little less. Then once in a while he would say, "You don't trust me."

I don't remember if I verbalized this or not, but I surely thought, "You bet your Red Rider I don't trust you." That's such a chicken-and-the-egg thing! The teenager says to the parent, "You don't trust me." The parent keeps replying to the teenager, "But you're not trustworthy," an endless cycle. I really believe it is up to the parent to break that cycle. Trust one more time. So you get burned. Trust one more time. Sooner or later, success will come. I don't believe the principle of forgiving one another at least 490 times (seventy times seven, as Christ told Peter) applies only to outsiders.

Tim once took a toy airplane from a store without paying for it. After we found out about it, we made him go back to the store and pay the owner for the airplane he had taken. I'm sure that was one of the hardest things Tim ever did, but he grew from that experience. And I'm sure the owner was impressed.

One of the things that changed Tim's life was a study in Proverbs. He did something that caused us to ground him from driving his car. I told him he could drive his car again if he would go through the Book of Proverbs, write out in longhand every verse that had the word "son" in it, and then explain to me what it meant. He took his Bible to school, worked on it after he got home, studied and worked and wrote and finally one morning at 6:30 A.M. he got me up and wanted to give his report. He began to go through the verses, and right away I noticed he had missed a couple. After I pointed this out he said, "You mean I have to do them even if they don't apply?"

Of course, the ones he missed were the very ones he needed, and the ones that applied the most to his situation. He returned to the Bible and in a few days came back with the project completed. We sat there, with tears streaming down our faces, as he explained what the Bible said about a rebellious attitude and some other struggles he was having. He wrote us later that summer, asking us to forgive him for his "tongue," and told us how much that Proverbs study had meant, now that he had had some time to really think about it.

If you have teenagers, it would be good to allow them to see what God's idea is of being a son. The same would work for a girl too. Just have her substitute the word *daughter* where Proverbs says *son*. The principles are still the same.

The writer of Proverbs said, "Don't fail to correct your children" (23:13, 14). This means we will have to get up out of our easy chairs, or from behind our newspapers, and take a trip somewhere—perhaps the bathroom or bedroom or basement or backyard—to make sure that loving correction remains current. It takes time to be a parent.

These verses also suggest that we keep short accounts on problems that need correcting. In this way the child will learn your guidelines and principles through a lot of small situations rather than a few giant blow-ups, which actually drive the child further into rebellion. If we do not discipline our children, they will grow up to be selfish, violent, angry adults.

Our prisons are full of the fruits of parents who set no limits, gave no time and no love.

Discipline helps the child to learn. One of the most common pictures in my mind as I reflect on newspaper and TV coverages of murders, rapes, and other violent crimes is the mother denying the guilt of her son or daughter—weeping—destroyed that anyone could accuse her "baby" of such a thing. The anguish of soul would be hard to imagine unless we have lived through that sort of thing.

I wish I could talk with each father in America, face to face, and share with him the hundreds of Scriptures that indicate that love is action, not feelings, and that it is not based on performance. The rejection of fathers could very well be the greatest reason for kids going wrong and falling into trouble. Show me a kid with a poor self-image, a rebellious spirit, a troublemaker, and I'll show you a dad who probably didn't care.

It is unfortunate that we have to rear children while we're trying to get careers off the ground, but that is the way it is. For those short growing-up years, we have to be full-time fathers and part-time workers. Then later, when the kids leave the nest, we will have plenty of time to work and play, and if we've done our job, the mother will have nothing but healthy pride in her sons and daughters.

I've talked with so many parents who are still struggling with their children, and the "kids" are in their thirties now, much too late to do anything but weep over their problems. Paul wrote:

And now a word to you parents. Don't keep on scolding and nagging your children, making them angry and resentful. Rather, bring them up with the loving discipline the Lord himself approves, with suggestions and godly advice (Ephesians 6:4).

This verse cautions us with a principle I see throughout the whole of Scripture, which is balance. It is all right to discipline. In fact, God requires that of us. But then let it go, forgive, and don't keep on nagging and scolding. Have some fun. Change the subject. Go camping—do something to show the children that you really do care, and that discipline is only for a moment to guide them. They may not understand until years later, but they will thank you for it eventually.

Continued scolding and nagging does result in rebellious kids because they finally come to the point of saying, "What's the use? Nothing I do is quite good enough. My parents are always giving me trouble for something."

We need to praise our kids as often as possible. I guess Tim's room was a good example. Barb and I had a little conflict over it, as she thought everything should pretty well be picked up. I felt that if Tim wanted to live in a messy room, it was all right. Everyone needs his space. Every so often Tim would attempt to clean his room. After he had worked for a while, he would call us to inspect. We first noticed all the things he hadn't done. The junk under the bed, the closet stuffed to the ceiling. We really blew it. What we should have done was praise him for the right things he had done. Had we done this, do you know what he would have done? Cleaned it again sometime. If I had praised him for taking out the garbage that one time, he would have taken it out again. We just have to be careful not to be looking always for the negative, but try to seek out the positive. When kids receive constant criticism, they give up, become bitter, resentful, and angry, which causes all kinds of problems for everyone.

One time we were waiting in an airport, and this little two-year-old chunk of a girl was hopping up and down, up and down, up and down. She had been waiting quite a while for the plane to come in, and was doing her best to keep herself entertained. All at once her mother glared at her and in a rage said, "Would you stop jumping!" There were only 437 people around, planes, intercoms, and other noise. The little girl wasn't disturbing anyone. It just bugged her mother that anyone could be happy, I guess. I just wanted to shake that mother and ask her what difference it made whether or not that little girl jumped. She was actually being very patient, waiting there with the older folks. Two-year-olds jump. That's the way God designed them. Yet we parents do all sorts of stupid things in the name of correction and discipline when it is usually to solve our own frustrations and anger. And innocent kids suffer. If that child continues to be stomped on like that the rest of her life, make room for her in one of our institutions. Her self-image won't be worth zilch, and hurting people do all kinds of crazy things to cope with hurts.

The key to child-rearing is for us to be in the Word, learning God's principles of joy, peace, love, self-control, and kindness. When we are in the Word, we become wise. Then God will speak through us, and our children will be blessed by our living Christ in front of them, showing unconditional love. Those are easy words to put down on paper, but hard to put into practice.

The writer of Proverbs said, "Teach a child to choose the right path, and when he is older he will remain upon it" (Proverbs 22:6). I had always been taught that this verse meant that if a child is trained in the things of the Lord, even if he strays away for a while when he is young, he will return to the faith when he is older. I've seen this at work. Many of the people who are now coming into our lives as new Christians have had some kind of spiritual background, even if very slight. A praying mother, a Sunday school teacher, a youth worker, an uncle, a neighbor—someone had exposed them to some of God's principles in early life, and now they are returning to Christ after some years of exile. And what joy we have as we see Christ touch a life after long years of neglect and rebellion!

We need to know our children so well that we can sense God's purpose, God's design in their lives. Some kids are born artists, some musicians, some mechanics, some philosophers, some organizers, some servants, some performers, some salesmen, some clowns, some serious. When we see God's design, we can guide our children along the path of their interests and gifts, helping them select the proper schools, classes, hobbies. It is tragic to see kids forced into the parents' mold, as the frustrated football father who forces his artistic son to become a linebacker. When the son fails, the father becomes bitter and angry. The frustrated piano player mother forces her daughter to labor long hours over a piano when the daughter's design and interest is painting.

Those of us who are parents would do ourselves a favor right now if we rededicated ourselves to being positive with our kids, praising them, honoring them, asking their forgiveness when we have hurt them, accepting them, talking to them—not at them—listening to them, really listening. We should put ourselves in their shoes, feel what they are feeling, hurt when they hurt, cry when they cry, laugh when they laugh. Kids are a gift from God. Like all special gifts, they should be handled with the greatest of care.

TEN

66 How to Lose It All— and Become Rich 99

Becoming a servant was not what I had in mind for my life. My nature is to be served—not to serve others. I like to have things done my way, on my timing, and I don't appreciate a whole bunch of people running around with opinions different from mine.

I wouldn't have any conflict or problems in my life if people would only keep their opinions to themselves and let me do it my way. That's my nature, and what a shock it was when I discovered that God wanted me to do just the opposite—to serve others! *I qualify!*

Servants aren't supposed to own very much, and that bothered me also. I had heard someone say that God would take care of all my needs through his riches in Christ, and I took that to mean mostly financial. Since God was committed to meeting my financial needs, I assumed I would never miss a payment or a meal. And we never did, just like he said. However, we never had any extra, either. I knew I had thirty days' grace on my insurance policies, so one month I would delay one twenty-five days and then pay it, the next month I would delay one of the others twenty-five days and then pay it. Maybe the next month I would delay the light bill a few days, or stall the telephone bill a week or so. We never missed a meal. We never missed a payment, but, as I said, we had nothing left over, either.

The minute we got ahead thirty or forty dollars, the washer would quit, or a tire would blow out, or Christmas would come, or the kids would want a whole hamburger—not just half as in the olden days. What a shock to my budget!

God really did meet our needs. After a few years of this, I began to assume that it was not spiritual to have anything left over at the end of the month. One of my problems, of course, was that I didn't spend any time in the Word, so I assumed God wanted us poor or at least to just get by. I had heard of another verse that said money was the root of all evil. Later I found that it was "the love of money" and not the money itself that was evil. Then one day I ran into one of the most startling groups of verses I had ever read:

But remember this—if you give little, you will get little. A farmer who plants just a few seeds will get only a small crop, but if he plants much, he will reap much. Every one must make up his own mind as to how much he should give. Don't force anyone to give more than he really wants to, for cheerful givers are the ones God prizes. God is able to make it up to you by giving you everything you need and more, so that there will not only be enough for your own needs, but plenty left over to give joyfully to others. . . . Yes, God will give you much so that you can give away much, and when we take your gifts to those who need them they will break out into thanksgiving and praise to God for your help (2 Corinthians 9:6-8, 11).

I couldn't believe what I was reading. God would not only meet our needs, but he would give us a surplus so we could give it away joyfully! And the more we gave away, the more he would make sure we had so that we could give more away. I was stunned. God didn't have a problem with people having money. It was what we did with the money that mattered.

I could see how easy it would be to fall into the trap of giving to get. The reason we give is because we see a need and we want to plant some seeds in people's lives. If we plant a few seeds, we'll get a small crop. If we plant lots of seeds, we'll get a large crop. But if our focus is how much we'll get out of the deal, I think it breaks the cycle. We give because that's what God would have us do. He brings people with needs into our lives. We meet it. He turns around and gives us more to give out in his name. It's not for our glory— it's for his glory. We are just stewards—managers.

How would we feel if the banker sent us a little note this week saying, "Dear customer: We have fallen in love with your money, so it is no longer yours. We are off to Hawaii. Thank you very much."

I wonder how God feels when we run off with his money? It isn't really ours—we are just the managers.

The last thing the world expects us to do is part with our money. The world says, "Keep it." God says, "Give it away." And when we do that, many of our non-Christian friends have to say to themselves, "There must be something to this Christianity bit if they give away their money."

We need to be sensitive to the physical needs of oth-ers, first to members of God's own family and then to those outside—our neighbors, the guy at work, a girl in the bridge club, the kid who needs shoes. James instructs us not to just say, "Be warm" or "Be fed." He expects us to do something about the need.

When I first started a business of my own, one of my first clients left us with an unpaid bill of $10,000. They came well recommended through one of the local TV stations, but they simply walked away, saying they could not pay their bill. It was a terrible amount of money to lose, especially as I was just starting out in business. I could have told the stations that my client walked away, and we would not be able to pay the bill. The problem was that the stations had placed the time on our reputation—not the client's, so as a Christian, I felt that I had to repay the bills, even if the money came out of my own pocket. I wrote a letter to all the stations involved and explained the situation. I told them we would pay the bills, but could not do it very fast. We began sending $10 checks to a whole list of TV stations around the country. That must have looked very strange to them, to apply a $10 check toward a bill totaling thousands of dollars, but that is all we could do. We did that for several years until we had everyone paid off except a couple of stations in Seattle and Spokane.

Then one Christmas the stations in Seattle and Spokane forgave the remainder of the debt. We were so grateful! But paying on a bill that wasn't really ours may have done more to establish us as Christians in business than just about anything else we could have done.

A few years later something else happened that helped establish us as being just a little bit different than the rest. I had inherited a client with the business when I bought it. He was spending around $300 a month. Over the next couple of years, I showed him that electronic advertising worked, and his budget grew to $100,000 a month. Since I have always been a bit of a worrier, I was concerned that as soon as I got him spending some money, a bigger agency would come along and steal him away.

Sure enough, one day the ad manager came out to the office and announced that they were going to another agency in town. I won't go into all the details because some of the people are still around, but let me say that not only did I feel stabbed in the back, the media people who serviced our agency thought the same thing. They were expressing terribly bitter feelings toward this client for what he had done to me. I wrote about forty letters to people who were affected by the change, thanking them for service in the past and asking them not to be bitter, because I wasn't. Since God owned the agency, he could bring clients in and he could allow them to leave. My job was to do the very best possible work for my clients and if someone came along who could do it better, or for any reason a client wanted to make a change, that was his privilege and I would accept that as coming from God, believing that he had something better in mind.

I received some very interesting comments on my letter. I'm sure many of the sales reps didn't really understand what I was saying, but they accepted the fact that I was marching to a different drummer and loved me anyway. Later, when we were in the midst of buying our home and God brought in a better client to help pay for it, these same sales reps scratched their heads in amazement as to how things "worked out." Several of my non-Christian friends called and said, "That wasn't an accident, was it?" I assured them that at least from my standpoint it wasn't. God simply had a better situation in mind for us, and used that little episode to test whether we really had given the agency to him.

I have complete confidence that God has my best interest in mind, and whatever comes into my life will be filtered through his fingers of love. He knows all about it, and if I fit into his plans, everything works out for my good—that's his promise. I wouldn't trade that assurance and peace for all the money, fame, or status this world could give. And I've tasted a bit of each in those areas, so it's not just sour grapes.

When Barb and I were first motivated to tithe, we decided to give 11 percent rather than 10 percent. We figured that the people in the Old Testament looked at 10 percent as a minimum, and we had so much more because of Christ, we thought 11 percent would be a better figure at which to begin.

We began to make out "God's check" first. When we did, we were amazed. He helped us manage our 89 percent better than we ever did the 100 percent. We ran into more sales, and I just know that the car and refrigerator didn't break down as much as before. About that time, we had some supermarket sponsors at the TV station where I worked. After the grocery items had been used under the hot lights, they could not be returned to the store, so they were given to those of us who had been working on the set. We would split the "spoils" between those of us on the floor, and wouldn't you know, I had to go out and rent a freezer locker to hold all the hams, lunchmeat, bread, and other things the Lord was giving us to bring home. Isn't that just like the Lord to give an abundance when we honor and obey him?

As our salary grew over those first years, we kept the percentage the same. But our giving grew with our salary increases. Since God owned everything, he decided to begin giving us a surplus so we could give it away. We don't worry now about percentages other than as a check on our giving. We just meet the needs that God puts in our path and expect him to make sure we have plenty to give away. That doesn't mean someday I might not be on welfare, or lose the business. The economy might fail, but I don't worry about those things. The Psalmist wrote:

Oh, the joys of those who do not follow evil men's advice, who do not hang around with sinners, scoffing at the things of God; but they delight in doing everything God wants them to, and day and night are always meditating on his laws and thinking about ways to follow him more closely. They are like trees along a river bank bearing luscious fruit each season without fail. Their leaves shall never wither, and all they do shall prosper (Psalm 1:1-3).

A person who is grounded in God's Word on a continuing basis will prosper in anything he does. The Psalmist said of righteous men: "All they do shall prosper" (v. 3). Prosperity, I believe, could include financial as well as emotional and spiritual prosperity. It seems to me that God has no reason not to bless us financially if our focus is to serve others and give his money away.

I've known some Christians involved in schemes who seem to have the wrong focus. Their goal was money, money, money—more of it, bigger houses, cars, vacations, boats, and more money. I also know some people who are in the business to help other people by giving money away, and I would expect those people to prosper.

I guess Barb and I are a little gun-shy because of three separate occasions in the last few years when we have been called by people to give them "financial counseling." Since this is one of the areas we feel we have some God-given insights, we are always open to helping people with financial problems and priorities. These people sounded desperate to get together, and even though we were about to go out of our minds with deadlines and pressures, we arranged to meet them, only to find out that they wanted us to be involved in their business of pyramid selling. I really resented being used in this way. I'm sure God can use this type of thing in some people's lives if their focus is serving rather than getting; but one of the biggest problems is that every new person met becomes a prospect and, rather than encouraging friendships, they cause people to duck when they see them coming so they won't be snared.

Don't misunderstand—there is nothing inherently wrong with big cars, nice homes, diamonds, furs, swimming pools, and country club memberships—if used in the right way. These things become ministering currency and they can allow us to relate to a particular strata of society so we can share Christ with these needy people too. It works so long as God owns it all and we're just his servants, his stewards, his managers. He gives us the tools to minister to people in a variety of mission fields, such as in the tennis club, where there are a great many hurting people, believe it or not.

There is a difference between stewardship and ownership, we learned. I used to give God his 11 percent and thought he would be deliriously happy, because I knew some people who only gave a dollar or so.

When I turned my business over to God, my material goods, family, future, bank account, and time, he began to trust me with a little extra. We must be careful not to fall into the trap of giving to get, saying, "Here is everything I own, now shower me with the blessings you promised." We are to present everything to God because that's what he wants us to do. And then he showers us with blessings beyond what we would dare to dream or think, with a purpose of sharing the blessings with others. But a word of caution: I also believe God has designed some people to have less, by this

ME!

world's standards, so they can relate to non-Christians who are in the same situation.

There is another group of people who are constantly in financial trouble by giving away too much. These people are not paying their rent, or car payment, or feeding their families properly, or keeping up on their own obligations. Someone comes into their life who is in need and they give away what they don't have. I think that is contrary to what the Bible teaches. We can be irresponsible givers as well as being the kind of givers God honors. It is all a matter of priorities and balance and staying close to God's Word so he can give directions for day-to-day living.

I've noticed that almost always givers are married to savers. It's very important that we work out a balance in marriage. We suggest that couples have one family checking account where all the income checks are deposited, no matter who earns them. Then both the husband and wife should have separate accounts as well so that they do not have to be accountable to the other for what they do with it. Each payday a certain amount is given to each partner to deposit in his or her personal account for golf games, hairdos, or just to blow without feeling guilty.

God gave his people some specific instructions about how to handle their finances: "He will open to you his wonderful treasury of rain in the heavens, to give you fine crops every season. He will bless everything you do; and you shall lend to many nations, but shall not borrow from them" (Deuteronomy 28:12). Even though this was addressed to the Jews of the Old Testament, I think we can apply the principle today. God wants to bless us. And I believe this includes financial blessings. When God can trust us with money, then he gives us a treasury out of which we can give to others. In this verse, he is providing enough money to lend and that means our own bills are probably paid. He also suggests that we are not to borrow. In other words, it is better to lend than to borrow. That's why it is a good idea for a Christian to be debt free if at all possible, and that includes the mortgage on the house. One of the reasons to be debt free is so a Christian can better weather a financial downturn, but it also frees up funds to loan or preferably to give away.

Solomon wrote: "Just as the rich rule the poor, so the borrower is servant to the lender" (Proverbs 22:7). A person who owes money is often ill at ease around the lender. He is always on the borrower's mind, since he feels the need to pay back. Sometimes he or she is even resentful about having to borrow, and feels the lender is somehow at fault. Loaning money is a great way to lose friends.

Christ spoke often about money, perhaps more than about any other one subject. He said:

And if you are untrustworthy about worldly wealth, who will trust you with the true riches of heaven? And if you are not faithful with other people's money, why should you be entrusted with money of your own? For neither you nor anyone else can serve two masters. You will hate one and show loyalty to the other, or else the other way around—you will be enthusiastic about one and despise the other. You cannot serve both God and money (Luke 16:11-13).

This passage does not say that we cannot serve God and have money. It says we can't serve God and serve money. In other words, we are not to make money our focus and goal, our number one priority.

Do you want money? Then give it away. Do you want poverty? Then try to keep the money you have. If we can earn $10,000 a year, we long for $20,000. If we make $20,000, we feel we just *have* to make $30,000. Then we feel we can't make our payments unless we can earn $50,000. This ought to say something to us about how much satisfaction money in itself can bring us.

I'm thankful that God has given money to the kind of people who give it away. Their doing so means that God's work on earth can continue to function. Paul wrote:

But how shall they ask him to save them unless they believe in him? And how can they believe in him if they have never heard about him? And how can they hear about him unless someone tells them? And how will anyone go and tell them unless someone sends him? (Romans 10:14, 15).

I know a lot of "senders." God has blessed them greatly with money so they can give it away to people who are going out to win people to Christ and to minister in his name. There simply would not be any Christian organizations around if God also did not give some people the means to support them. This is just another proof that to be poor is not necessarily to be spiritual.

If we are the managers of God's funds, his stewards, God owns our money. All we have to do is distribute it for him. Paul wrote:

Do you want to be truly rich? You already are if you are happy and good. After all, we didn't bring any money with us when we came into the world, and we can't carry away a single penny when we die. So we should be well satisfied without money if we have enough food and clothing. But people who long to be rich soon begin to do all kinds of wrong things to get money, things that hurt them and make them evil-

*minded and finally send them to hell itself. For the
love of money is the first step toward all kinds of sin.
Some people have even turned away from God because
of their love for it, and as a result have pierced themselves with many sorrows* (1 Timothy 6:6-10).

This may be the verse that gives people the idea that
it is spiritual to be poor. It is true—we didn't bring any
money with us into this world, and we won't take any
with us when we die. It is said that a friend of John D.
Rockefeller was asked, after the rich man died, "How
much money did Rockefeller leave, anyway?" The answer: "All of it!"

The Apostle Paul said that he could be content in
plenty or want, just as long as he had enough food and
enough clothing. People whose focus is money do all
kinds of things to get more, including cheating. But Jesus said, "What profit is there if you gain the whole
world—and lose eternal life?" (Matthew 16:26).

It is going to be a terrible shock to a lot of people
who will stand on the other side of the gulf, realizing
that they chose the wrong path—that leads to destruc-
tion rather than eternal life through Christ. I can almost hear the scoffers now crying, "Foolishness!" And
sad as it is, many of these people will not know they
have made the wrong choice until they stand before
the Judge and hear God say, "I never knew him. Take
him away."

Wealth often keeps a person from doing what God
wants him to do. The striving after riches can be all-
consuming and distract terribly from ministering to
others. Paul wrote that "those in frequent contact with
the exciting things the world offers should make good
use of their opportunities without stopping to enjoy
them; for the world in its present form will soon be
gone" (1 Corinthians 7:31). I know Christians who are
professional athletes, movie stars, well-known politi-

cians, authors, TV personalities—people in the public
eye. Some of them have received gifts from the Lord
of mansions, luxury cars, huge bank accounts, investments, successful businesses, swimming pools, tennis
courts, country club memberships, and other things
that might not appear as "needs" to the average person. Yet these same people make good use of the opportunities this status—position, fame, and wealth—
gives them to share Christ with non-Christians. But the
Bible warns Christians who are so blessed not to stop
too long to enjoy these "good" things, but to keep
going with the goal in mind of reaching as many hurting people for Christ as they possibly can, and staying
in the center of God's will in everything they do.

The Christians in professional sports have a particu-
larly effective platform from which to witness. The
world worships sports heroes, and if they say to kids,
"Drugs—that's where it's at," then the kids will try
drugs. If they say, "Life with Christ is where it's at,"
then the kids will be more open to Christ.

There is absolutely nothing wrong with having the
nice things this world offers as long as God owns
them and they are being used to honor him and his
people. Almost anything can be used to serve God if
having it is appropriate to how he wants us to live.

I had breakfast recently with a young man who was
going through deep water financially. He had been vac-
illating back and forth between jobs ever since I'd
known him. That in itself was not wrong. God put me
through a variety of jobs in order for me to gain experience. In fact, I suspect he may not be done with me
yet. This man seemed to think that since he is now a
Christian, God owed him more money, as a reward for
getting into the Word, attending our class and church,
exposing himself to Christian fellowship. *Surely God
will reward my dedication*, he thought.

God does want to give us good gifts. His desire is to

give us beyond what we could ask or dream of. But God does not owe us anything. Contentment with what we have may be one of the most elusive things we strive for. No, the grass is *not* greener on the other side of the fence. So why do we keep looking at it? Longing for it? Striving for it? Killing ourselves to get over there and taste some of it? I suppose one reason might be our goals and what we want out of life.

I'm a master goal-setter. I have goals for this afternoon, tomorrow, next year—even goals for when I retire. The logical thing for me to do when I accomplish a goal is to set another goal, of course. It is often hard for me to sit down and enjoy what I have. I always have another goal in mind and my attention shifts to that.

I have an elaborate exercise gym out in the garage that I have used ten times or so. Now, before you criticize, I bought it to put in the basement, but it wouldn't fit, so I had to put it out in the cold, freezing, dark, damp garage. I open myself up to pneumonia traveling all the way from our house to the garage to work out, so I don't go out there often. I guess I could knock a hole in our kitchen floor to allow room for the thing to stick up from the basement. I'll ask Barb about that later, or maybe I should just do it sometime when she's at Bible study to surprise her.

I also have some workshop tools that I have never assembled. Bev, my daughter, mentioned once that she would like to learn woodworking, so I invested in some machinery, only I lost interest after it arrived, and I haven't gotten it set up yet. But I will. Don't be impatient.

Obviously God is not jumping up and down with delight about this tendency of mine to reach for a goal, attain it, and then go for another without first really stopping to enjoy the first one. It is important that I be reminded once in a while that God wants me to be satisfied and not always to be scrambling for another goal.

I make Barb tired. In fact, in one of our recent arguments, she blurted out, "I haven't had a moment's rest since the day I met you!"

Now that's simply not true. That's just an emotional message. I remember clearly on May 14, 1963, when she was able to relax and then again on August 20, 1970. It was a wonderful day of relaxation for her. So how can she make a statement like that? Solomon wrote:

O God, I beg two favors from you before I die. First, help me never to tell a lie. Second, give me neither poverty nor riches! Give me just enough to satisfy my needs! For if I grow rich, I may become content without God. And if I am too poor, I may steal, and thus insult God's holy name (Proverbs 30:7-9).

Someone has said that wealth is a by-product of the righteous activity of those who do not seek it. One of the greatest traps for people with money might be for them to think they had something to do with attaining it. If it came through their talents, their abilities were God's handiwork. If they inherited it, God put them in that particular family. If they were in the right place at the right time, God put them in that place. We have no right to be proud of our money, which will soon be gone, anyway. We should go about doing good deeds with our money—sharing, giving, loving, reaching out to those in need. That is how treasure is accumulated—in heaven. We can have a wonderful life down here, doing good and serving others with our money, and a better life with Christ someday for eternity. Who could want anything more?

It is amusing sometimes to hear people fighting with their circumstances. They say that they are God's servants, but when the proper amount of money fails to come in, their car breaks down, they lose their job, or someone gets sick or dies, then they have all sorts of suggestions for God as to how he should handle their situation. We step in and get all bent out of shape, take things into our own hands, worry, fight the circumstances, take the burden ourselves. I've found in my own life that when God is involved in a situation, the answers come on God's timetable, not mine. If we try to force the door open, and it opens, it may not necessarily be from God. He might just step aside and let us handle it on our own. And we don't need to be reminded of what could happen then.

God has many ways to pay for his ministries. The Apostle Paul was a Christian who happened to be a tentmaker, just as I feel that I am a Christian who just happens to be in advertising. I'm thankful that God has given me a successful business that generates profits to give away and to pay for our ministries, travel, meals, conferences, books, and counseling expenses related to our ministries. We are absolutely free to do exactly what God wants us to do because he is supplying the money through our business. We do not have to ask for support.

I see so many of the people in Christian organizations who become distracted from their ministry because they seem to be constantly behind financially and have to go out and raise more money. Just this week I received a letter from a well-known Christian organization saying they were in deep trouble because they had expanded their ministry and now couldn't pay for it and wanted us to help out. Was God really involved in the expansion? I had no indication from God that I should respond.

One of the things that bothers me most is getting emergency letters from organizations, over and over and over again. It seems as if they never have enough money to run their ministry. I get steely cold when I read for the umpteenth time that a particular ministry is in trouble. My first thought is bad management—poor stewardship of the funds God has already given them—because God isn't broke, and one of the ways he directs is through finances. If the money for a particular ministry is not coming in on time, then I think we need to take another look at the ministry to see if we have missed something. There are exceptions, of course, but I guess I resent the letters that imply, "If you don't send us your check today, we'll be out of business, or have to call back some missionaries, or go off the radio, or we won't be able to build the new building."

Brother, let me say this in love. It probably is God's plan for you to go off the air, or not build the building, or let the missionaries come home. He will supply the funds if he is in the project. It would not be logical for him to do otherwise. You don't have to agree. This has just been my experience.

I guess if I were building an organization I would start with one person and a ministry of some kind. Then when that person got so busy he couldn't see, then I would hire another one. Then when both people were running in circles, I would hire another. As God provided the funds to pay for the people and the projects, I would expand the camps, youth work, mission, evangelistic outreach—whatever. If this was God's project, he would provide the funds. If it was not his project, I would expect him to cut off the funds, forcing me to cut back until I was all alone again. And then I would go out and play tennis, or change my direction, knowing God owns all the money in the universe. He can provide funds for ministries if the people and focus are in the center of his will.

Some people have a problem with Christians making a profit. In reading Matthew 25:14-30, which I won't quote here, I believe there is a principle taught that shows that making a profit is not wrong. In fact, a profit is expected by God. The story in Matthew speaks for itself. A reasonable profit is not a sin. Actually it is the means whereby a business can expand, pay its employees, and repay the stockholders who have taken a risk by investing in the business when it began. I don't believe in excessive profits—again the word balance—not too much, not too little.

A guy at the TV station where I worked was a fantastic tape operator. He was always ready. He had great ideas. He worked hard, and had a cheerful attitude. There was another guy at the master control who did nothing but read the paper and gripe, was undependable, was a poor worker, and had a bad attitude. The union said we had to pay them both the same—a tragedy in my opinion. The guy at the tape machine soon lost his incentive to work hard since he was not getting more pay than the guy who was lazy and grouchy. There's nothing wrong in paying people according to the gifts God has given them and for the work they do.

There is nothing wrong in receiving a fair profit. There is nothing wrong in being paid for our abilities. It's not what we have—it's what we do with what we have that counts for eternity. Paul wrote:

Pay everyone whatever he ought to have: pay your taxes and import duties gladly, obey those over you, and give honor and respect to all those to whom it is due. Pay all your debts except the debt of love for others—never finish paying that! For if you love them, you will be obeying all of God's laws, fulfilling all his requirements (Romans 13:7, 8).

Several versions and translations read: "owe no man anything," which makes it sound as if we should never borrow for anything. *The Living Bible* is more accurate with the Greek, which means "don't keep on owing." In other words, pay your bills promptly and fully. Personally, I see nothing wrong even in using credit cards if you pay them off every month. I realize some will probably spend more because they have them, but if God is directing their spending, I see nothing wrong in making use of the convenience of "plastic money."

Sometimes we prevent God from meeting our needs when we go ahead and buy on credit rather than waiting for him to provide for us. That is something we should consider when we think about borrowing.

The two keys to handling finances God's way are first of all *ownership*, making sure that God is the owner of our money, and that we are just the managers. Second, we must consider ourselves *servants*, which involves giving money away to those who need it.

There may not be a more effective witness than the person who gives his or her money away, looking after the needs of others—not just himself. One of the most loving things we can do is help a person financially as God directs our path.

The world says, "Keep it!" God says, "Give it away." He will make sure your barns are full and your bank accounts overflowing so that you can give it away joyfully, and others can see that your deeds are as good as your doctrine. Words without deeds are empty shells. When we give God 100 percent ownership of our finances, we can then stand back and watch him bless!

ELEVEN
66 What about Church? 99

Church was just something we did every week when I was growing up. I'm thankful for my parents' faithfulness in making me go to church, but as far as relating to my everyday life, it didn't. When we would go out to visit on Sunday afternoon, we were not allowed to play ball, read comics, or do any fun things. We just sat around in our "church clothes" and felt miserable.

My parents weren't that way. They gave us lots of freedom, but when we went out, they wanted us to conform to other people's rules and honor them, a biblical principle I did not learn until many years later. I can hear some of you saying, "Why force a kid to go to church and be miserable?"

Well, going to church as a family and being exposed to spiritual things is essential, in my opinion, to set the foundation of a life, even if the kids don't fully understand or enjoy it. Even now, not all church services meet my needs. But meeting my needs is not the only reason I should attend. I believe we have a responsibility to be examples to people around us, to encourage them, honor them, and we can't do that if we are not there. Many times we have to just forget our own needs—put them aside—with a view to being with others when they have needs. Yes, we should force our kids to go to church with us, despite all the hassles, knowing that someday the child will turn thirteen or so and announce that he no longer will be attending church with us.

That will be a crisis time. Any wavering on our part and the battle is lost. It's one thing to go walk in the park when the baby has hiccups. It's another to leave him home to watch TV. If the child is a member of the family, he will do what the family does. And that means go to church, whether he likes it or not, until around the age of eighteen or so, depending on the maturity of the child. Then release him to make his own decision, taking the risk that he might not go to church.

Ideally, we should make our church programs so appealing that the kids (and adults) can't wait to get to church, whether it is Sunday morning, evening, AWANA, Pioneer Girls, or whatever. The young people's program of the church needs to rate right up there among the very highest priorities of the congregation. Yet too often it is relegated to the basement, in more ways than just physically.

I can't even remember if we had a youth minister at any of the churches I attended while growing up, or at the ones I attended during the summers when I worked on my grandparents' farm. I started driving a wheat truck when I was nine years old and worked on the farm every summer until I was twenty.

We didn't go to church very often during the summer. Sunday was the only day off I had, and I didn't have the heart to blow a perfectly good day in church. When we did go, I was a bit frightened, because it was a charismatic church, and the people made more noise than I was used to hearing. So I stayed away as much as I could.

When I went away to college, the church meant even less to me. I went very little until the semester after Barb and I were married. When we returned to the campus after our honeymoon, I had this feeling that church was supposed to be important, so we would go to the 11:00 A.M. service, and then leave as quickly as we could and get back to our own little apartment. After graduation, we left for our two-year hitch in the army, had our first child, and somehow (probably from the good foundation both sets of parents gave us) felt that a church had to be a part of our lives in some way.

After we settled into our army housing, we were driving around one day and saw a sign calling attention to Snyder Memorial Baptist Church. The name somehow attracted us, so we decided one Sunday to try it. The sun was shining warmly that day as we approached this beautiful brick church with a Southern-style white steeple, just like those we had seen in magazines. As we left the morning service, we were surrounded by young couples our own age, many of them army couples with whom we had much in common. They invited us to get involved socially with their young married's class. I never have been socially outgoing, but we accepted one of the first invitations to a social, got to the church, looked in the window at the group of people having fun. But we had a small baby in our arms and felt out of place, so we went home. I'm sure it was not Barb's choice to go home, since she had more self-confidence, but she was willing to let me take the lead. Eventually we did become involved with the class and then began teaching a children's evening session called Training Union.

Something began to happen at this church. I could understand what the minister was saying, and what he said came close to meaning something to my everyday life. I began to look forward to Sunday and the people I met. Barb and I began to feel a part of that body. Then tragedy struck! Our young pastor announced that he was leaving to take a pulpit in another city. I was absolutely devastated. How could he do this to us? But he did, and my memory goes dim after that from a spiritual standpoint until we came home from the army.

After we returned home, we stayed with both sets of parents for a time while I looked for a job. I knew I wanted to be in television, so I turned down a couple of jobs in radio, hoping something in TV would open up. In the meantime we attended church with the folks. But since we did not have any roots, it was hard to get involved in a new fellowship very fast.

After we settled in Seattle, my Mom mentioned having played the piano in a certain church there and suggested we try that one. We attended one Sunday, and were immediately accepted and made to feel welcome. We attended that church for about six years. Then a group of people who didn't like the doctrine the pastor was preaching began to take steps against him, which included legal action. Finally they brought the activities of the church to a halt through the courts. I wasn't into the Bible at that time and was not acquainted with how blatantly that action violated scriptural principles.

I became a member of the group supportive of the pastor. We met to decide what to do about the matter. We had a unity of mind, and following the pastor's lead, we left the church in a body, giving the group who had made so much trouble the facilities, the equipment, the furniture—everything. We didn't even take a paper clip, as our pastor reminded us so often later. We began meeting in a school, and I can remember the excitement of having a common bond once again. Some people would bring the hymnals, some the nursery equipment, some the Sunday school materials. Everyone pitched in to make the group function.

Then, little by little, dreams and plans of a new church building came to be and in 1964 we had the first service in our brand new church. What a day! The men of the church had put hours and hours of work on the structure. It was truly a monument to what could be done with a unity of mind and spirit.

I was the chairman of the finance committee. We sold bonds and paved parking lots. The Lord blessed the church greatly, both spiritually and financially. I was very active in the church, taught junior church, served on several committees and boards, and was active in our young married's class. I related well to our first Sunday school teacher and his wife. In the morning service I found myself under the ministry of a very dynamic preacher, who pounded the pulpit a little more than I liked. But I enjoyed much of what he had to say, as it seemed to make sense, even though I really wasn't all that interested in the Bible at that time.

I found myself a member of a lot of boards outside the church, too, but I sometimes felt a little out of place because I usually felt we should go ahead with a project in which the Lord seemed to be leading, even if we didn't know exactly how we were going to pay for it. I guess my feeling was that the leaders of the children of Israel probably had to put their feet into the water before the sea opened. So I felt we needed to step out in faith on some of the "impossible" projects we faced, and see if God would open the door.

Later I found out the real reason why I was so uncomfortable in board meetings. I don't have the gift of administration, as outlined in the Bible. No wonder I was so frustrated! I was trying to do something for which I was not gifted. It is a mistake to ask a person to serve on a board of trustees or deacons if the person doesn't have the gift of administration. Certainly, it would help to have an occasional man of faith on the board, too. It's wrong, for instance, to put a person in charge of the hospital ministry who doesn't have the gift of mercy. The head of the missions committee should have the gifts of mercy and giving. The chairman of the church should obviously have the gift of administration among other things. The effective Sunday school teacher needs to have the gift of teaching or exhortation. The spiritual leader of the church should have the gift of wisdom, among others. The finance chairman should probably have the gifts of faith and of giving. The kitchen committee head should have the gift of helps. The chairman of the outreach committee should have the gift of evangelism.

In a small church, matching gifts with jobs may not always be possible. But my point is that I have seen very little effort on the part of many churches to pick people for jobs according to their gifts and talents.

Barb and I taught junior church for eighteen years. We had a wonderful time with the kids. This was not just play time—you can ask any of our graduates. This was serious business. We had our own little pastor, song leader, deacons, deaconesses, trustees, ushers, and other church officers. They ran most of the service without any help from us. Barb or I would preach a "sermon" which was designed to their level and interest span.

We had to write most of our own material because there just wasn't much in the way of curriculum for fourth, fifth, and sixth grade junior church the way we

wanted to teach it. The material that was available was
mostly Bible stories, and we wanted a little more doctrine and practical application of the Word. We didn't
want our kids to be bored with church, so we tried
very hard to make it exciting. We treated them as
equals. They called us Chuck and Barb—none of this
Mr. and Mrs. Snyder bit, which separates young and
old. I don't mean that kids shouldn't show respect for
authority, but in a teaching situation, the teacher must
be real, vulnerable, and transparent, on the level of the
hearers. After Barb's or my talk, we would have an activity time, when we would play some rousing games.

I can't remember ever having a discipline problem.
There were a few kids, of course, who acted up once
in a while, but we would calmly explain to them that
they could not come back if they kept acting up, and
would have to sit with their parents in big church.
That did it! They became instant angels. They wanted
to come to junior church—they didn't have to. That's
the way it should be in big church, too. People should
want to come, not feel compelled to.

Then Barb decided to attend the morning service, so
now I had to give the lesson. Since the Bible was not
practical to my life, I looked for my material in books
and prepared lessons or used some of Barb's material.
Most of it had Scripture in it, but it didn't mean all
that much to me. The kids learned something, I know,
because I watched them grow. But I didn't really take
anything home with me from church.

It was about that time that I attended the Basic
Youth seminar. For the first time in my life, I was motivated to begin looking in the Bible on my own for
things I could apply to my life. And immediately I began to sprout. The Bible began to be real and practical,
and people began dropping into my life who needed
the very things I was learning. That was about the time

I began reading some of the books Barb had been telling me about, and later became familiar with *The Living Bible*.

I became so excited and impressed with the practical Bible I had "discovered," I suggested we form a small group on Sunday mornings during the Sunday school hour where we could explore some of these new principles I had been learning. People signed up for the class and we began our pilgrimage along with other people who were eager to learn how to make the Bible real in their lives. This group grew until one summer we had about seventy people meeting with us.

I couldn't believe the excitement I sensed in that group! We were talking about revolutionary things, such as anger, depression, worry, being a servant, giving up our rights, anxiety, and stress, all bathed in the principles we were finding in Scripture relating to these problems. One man in his seventies, a leader in the church for years, came up to me one Sunday and said, "This is the first time in my life I have ever wanted to come to Sunday school." Isn't that the way it should be?

Remember, I don't take any credit for that. I told the Lord I was no teacher, and he agreed with me. The things that were happening were what God was teaching us when we accepted his Word as being a practical book for our lives.

About that time, Barb and I began teaching the young marrieds' class. The class became more and more exciting as people were caring, learning, loving, and growing together. Marriages were healed. People came to know Christ personally. The Bible became more real to all of us.

I took a survey in the young marrieds' class we were teaching, asking them for confirmation on the practical way I was teaching. Quite a few of them wanted more doctrine rather than practical application, so again our roots were being loosened just a bit more as far as service in that particular church was concerned. This was God's hand, not man's.

Several things came up that led Barb and me to look for another place of ministry. I have nothing but the deepest respect and love for the people at our other church, but we sensed God was pushing us along to another place. God is the author of change in our lives. He can open and shut doors as he wants to.

During the time of our ministry at the other church, more and more of the pro athletes in town began dropping into our lives. We met Jim Zorn of the Seattle Seahawks football team through a Cystic Fibrosis commercial he recorded with me. Because he was so open, it took Barb and me five minutes to discover he was a Christian. We took him to dinner and have been good friends ever since.

A local pastor asked us to have an athlete and media Bible study in our home and Jim brought his pastor. We were immediately impressed with the spirit of this man, and soon found ourselves visiting his church on the East side. Quite a few of the pro athletes attended that church and we felt God wanted us to be involved in their lives in some way, principally as friends. And I guess that has happened, because not too long ago we were attending a conference where the speaker was telling us how important it is to have friendships cutting across cultural, age, racial, and economic lines. One of our black athlete friends came up to us after the meeting and said, "You and Barb fulfill two of these requirements. You're our *old* white friends."

We are old enough to be their parents, so I think this has helped over the years to have the "kids" trust us.

Barb and I also serve as chaplains to the University of Washington football team. We travel with the team and do some counseling when it's needed. They have learned to trust us, too, because we love them right where they are, with no expectations—just be there. And little by little, they have begun to feel our love just as our pro athlete friends have.

We do not have a "ministry" to athletes. We simply have some friends who happen to be in that line of work. There are people called to minister to athletes, but we just want to be helpful friends. We also have friends who are in the media, some who are in advertising, some who are plumbers, some contractors— even some pastors. The word "ministry" bothers me a little. It seems to give the impression that someone is trying to force a relationship with someone else. It sounds like a one-way relationship to me. Our friends minister to us also. It's a wonderful two-way street.

As more and more of the people connected with athletics began coming into our lives, part of our reaction was a desire to worship where they worship, since they all lived on the East side and probably would never come over the bridge to church. Changing churches was threatening to Barb because she had to leave all her relationships built up over almost twenty years. However, the Lord gave her insight as to the reasons for the move.

As we sat in our new church, I kept reminding the Lord that we were there to serve in some way if he had something for us to do. I was content to just sit there and be fed, for I was taking three pages of notes every Sunday and really enjoying the fellowship. Then one day the pastor mentioned that the young marrieds' class needed a teacher and asked if Barb and I would take the class. My response was "Thank you, Lord," because it was a direct answer to prayer.

Very few of our friends from the other church really understood our leaving. I'm sure some felt rejected, but we felt "called" to this new church just as surely as if we had received a call to Africa or China, so we had to give their suspicions and reactions to the Lord and let him take care of them. About four years later one of the members from the old church told me how excited he was about our new relationships with young couples and athletes. I thanked him, and again shared my feelings about our leaving and the fact that some of the people still didn't understand. He answered, "I know, I was one of them, but I do now." What an encouragement it was to me!

As we began teaching this new class, more and more loving, caring, growing, sharing, supporting, giving people began attending, and all of a sudden I realized we were becoming a little "church." Not in the negative sense of being in competition, but in a positive way, we were becoming a microcosm of what the larger church should be.

In my reading I came across a couple of books that said some very wise things about what the church should be. It was as if these authors had a microphone in my head, because they were saying in print exactly what I had been thinking and what was happening in our class. Two of these books were *Love, Acceptance and Forgiveness* by Jerry Cook (Regal, 1979) and *Lifestyle Evangelism* by Joseph C. Aldrich (Multnomah, 1981), both of which I highly recommend. But of course, the most authoritative book ever written on the subject of the church is the Bible itself.

The Apostle Paul gave some important insights as to what should take place in church:

For I long to visit you so that I can impart to you the faith that will help your church grow strong in the Lord. Then, too, I need your help, for I want not only to share my faith with you but to be encouraged by yours: Each of us will be a blessing to the other (Romans 1:11, 12).

Paul wanted to come to Rome to give the people a spiritual message of some kind, a gift of faith or insight. As he thinks about his trip, he is also excited about the encouragement he is going to receive in return from his fellow Christians there. It is part of the church's job to encourage one another, support one another, believe in one another, and give unconditional love, so that all can be built up and then return to the outside world to fight the battles once more.

Paul wrote in another place: "He will give eternal life to those who patiently do the will of God, seeking for the unseen glory and honor and eternal life that he offers" (Romans 2:7). This verse first brings to mind an older lady in one of the churches Barb and I attended quite a few years ago. This lady stood by the door after every service, greeting the members, and paying special attention to strangers, making everyone feel wanted and accepted. We'll never read about her in *Christianity Today* or *Moody Monthly*. We will never see her on TV with Billy Graham—and honestly, I can't even remember her name, but I'll bet God does! She was not seeking to be noticed for what she was doing. Hers was this "unseen glory" Paul spoke about. Her mission was to patiently do God's will for her life, the simple little act of making people feel special. It is not our visibility that counts, contrary to what I observe in the lives of many pastors and Christian leaders with whom I have contact. It is our faithfulness to exercise our gifts, whatever they might be.

It is also possible to force ourselves into areas where spiritual gifts are required that we really don't have. I know an assistant pastor who thinks he has the gift of teaching. He gives it a good try, but the classes dwindle down and down in size until he decides to do

something else. He does do a good job of planning—
great ideas, good organizational ability—but instead of
going with his obvious gift of administration, he forces
his way into teaching situations. It makes it hard for
everyone concerned.

Sometimes this "unseen glory and honor" involves
outsiders who come into the church for some reason,
such as the time Barb and I hosted a wedding. As
hosts, we were by the back door. Right in the middle
of the service three dirty, shabby hippie-types slipped
into the church and stood there for a few minutes,
wondering whether to run or hide. I greeted them in a
soft voice so as not to disrupt the service, learned
their names, found a place for them to sit, and the
service went on. I talked with them during the recep-
tion as they stood all alone in one corner. But not one
person came up to greet them or made any effort to
make them feel welcome. They turned out to be
friends of the bride, and she was the only other person
in that entire group of several hundred people to even
smile at them or try to ease their obvious discomfort.

It was sad. People need to be overwhelmed with
love when they come into the church, no matter how
they look, smell, or act. That way, they might want to
come back, and their lives might be changed. Paul
taught other things about the church, showing who deserved to be there:

*Then what can we boast about doing, to earn our sal-
vation? Nothing at all. Why? Because our acquittal is
not based on our good deeds; it is based on what
Christ has done and our faith in him. So it is that
we are saved by faith in Christ and not by the good
things we do* (Romans 3:27, 28).

A common theme in all of the Bible shows clearly
that we can't earn salvation. But it doesn't stop there.

While there is nothing we can do to earn salvation, there are plenty of things we should want to do to show our appreciation for what God has done for us. Since we have eternal life through Christ, people should see the evidence of it in our lives. We should show a supernatural ability to handle our anger, temptations, trials, our tongues, and the other things that hamper our walk. If people don't ever see changes in our lives, they have reason to doubt that we really know Christ personally.

There is a difference between what we call "works" and exercising spiritual gifts. It is important to realize that even the neat talents God gives us require work. Someone with the gift of teaching needs to study hard; one with the gift of preaching should see that his sermons apply to his people's everyday lives. If God has trusted someone with this world's goods, he should be thankful, and then be wide open to using those gifts as ministering currency in other people's lives. Someone who likes systems and programs should work hard at supervising the work of the church or in business or other organizations that need good leadership. If someone has a special heart for the handicapped, the sick, the elderly, he should work hard at cheering them up. These are the types of gifts to strive for—those that will help other people. And speaking of people in need, Paul wrote: "When God's children are in need, you be the one to help them out. And get into the habit of inviting guests home for dinner, or if they need lodging, for the night" (Romans 12:13).

One of the best ways to get a non-Christian's attention is to help meet his needs. There wouldn't be the need for a welfare system if the church was doing its part.

Someone once asked a group of people how many of them thought the government would meet their needs if they needed help. About 90 percent of the

people responded yes. Then they were asked how
many thought the church would take care of their
needs in a crisis and only 5 percent said yes. What a
sad commentary! The church should be first in line to
help meet people's needs.

We can understand why some are reluctant to tell
others about their needs, whether spiritual, financial,
emotional, or material. Therefore we all need to listen
for hidden messages, watch for body language, and ask
appropriate questions to determine need. And then we
should follow up on our feelings. God will show what
our role should be in that person's life. That doesn't
mean we go around prying into the affairs of everyone
we meet. It just means that God will give us a special
sensitivity if we are open and looking for people to
help.

Recently we had five Athletes in Action basketball
players stay with us overnight. They went through several dozen cookies, stacks of pizza, gallons of pop—
but we received the great blessing of sharing with
them God's bountiful gifts to us. Even when we lived
in a very small house, we made a practice of having
two or three couples over for pie on Sunday nights.
We were church-mouse poor, but Barb is a good cook
and we had some fabulous fellowship around her wonderful pies. We learned that it doesn't have to be fan-
cy. It's the thought that counts in making people feel
special, wanted, and needed. And I suggest not limiting
yourself to just having the "beautiful people" over.
Make sure you include the lonely, depressed, and other
people who might not exactly fit your personality, but
who desperately need someone to love them unconditionally.

We have to be more than observers in the church—
we need to be doers, and in this case, doing something
to help friends in need. If someone has a flat tire on
the freeway, we should be the one to stop and help. If

a neighbor needs some money to pay his rent, we should be the one to reach out with some dollars. If we see someone who is lonely, we should be the one to comfort him. If we see someone who is downhearted, we should be the one to encourage. If we see someone struggling, we should be the one to come alongside and help.

Churches need to find the balance in what they believe and how they live—doctrine and practice. Even though most people tend to worship in churches and groups where they feel comfortable doctrinally, or attend because they have been reared in that particular fellowship, there are times when we have people among us who don't agree with some of our doctrine but enjoy the fellowship and want to remain a part of the group. I guess I can see both sides of having a person sign a doctrinal statement before joining a church. There is the possibility of division if there is too wide a gap in the doctrinal stand of members, and I do believe the people who teach in a particular church should agree with the position of the church on the major points of doctrine. This is all necessary and healthy.

I guess my dream church, however, would be one in which people of all kinds of doctrinal persuasions could worship, a place where they could be open to growing and learning and loving the people around them unconditionally, regardless of their beliefs. Since we're dealing with humans, it's only a nice dream, I suppose. There is no doubt that proper doctrine will allow us to be more successful in our own personal Christian life, which in turn makes us more attractive to non-Christians as we grow in grace and love toward others. The problem is that many of us stop short of applying our doctrinal beliefs. We need to practice what we preach.

In the Christian life, it is not enough to know what

we should do. We must put into practice what is right, doing good things for others, loving the unlovely, enduring trials and suffering, giving, being a servant. First, we get into the Word to get our feet set on the major doctrinal issues of Christianity. But then we must go out and live them, putting into practice those things we have learned, doing what we should do—not only those things we want to do.

And by the way, we need to live our Christianity when no one else is looking, too. For instance, not too long ago I bought some jewelry for Barb from a jeweler who heard our testimony and has seen me on TV. He knows we are Christians and has treated us special, even though I have no reason to think he is a Christian. Anyway, as we were working out the final details, he mentioned that if I had a friend in Oregon, he would be glad to send the jewelry to him, and he in turn could mail it to me in Seattle so we could save the sales tax, since there was no tax on goods shipped to an out-of-state address.

Earlier in my life, before I really began getting into the Bible, I might have been tempted, but I quickly said, "No, thanks. I really believe in supporting the government."

He, of course, agreed that I had made the right decision, and I paid the tax. However, with just a word, I could have saved myself some money. The jeweler is not dishonest—he is just caught up in the world's system, and that is what the world does. But Christians shouldn't do that, because we are told to honor the government and pay our taxes. I didn't put this guy down for offering to help me. He wanted to help me and I appreciated his offer of kindness.

A few months ago we discovered one of the radio stations on which we had been buying time for Safeway had made a mistake and was charging us too much for some spots we were running. I suggested they send Safeway a refund check, which they did. But it was made out to me—not to Safeway. No one would have been the wiser if I had simply deposited that check in my own account and praised the Lord for providing funds in such a wonderful way. The station had done its part. Safeway didn't know about the mistake. I was home free—except! I am a Christian and the Bible says I am not to steal. So without a moment's hesitation, I signed over the check to Safeway and sent it on to their advertising manager. Some might think I had a choice there, but I really didn't. If I'm going to practice being a Christian as the Bible instructs me to do, I can't steal, or lie, or be unfaithful to Barb, or take revenge, or get drunk, or ruin my body with bad habits, continue in lustful thoughts, be angry all the time, be disloyal to my friends, cheat on my income tax, slack off when my boss is not looking. These are principles from God's Book, and it's up to me to practice them. In fact, the Bible says that it is a sin if I know the right thing to do and then don't do it (James 4:17). Doctrine is important, but we must go out and live it. The greatest danger to the evangelical church is not communism or cults—it is the wide gap between what we say and how we live.

When we talk about church and churches, I think it is good to remember that a church is not a building. It is us, if we have Christ in our lives. *We* are the temple of the Holy Spirit—not the building where we meet. *We* are the church. That's why I get tired of "super-saints" complaining when part of the church building is used as a gymnasium, of all things! "Why, people could get sweaty! And who can worship in a place where people have sweated?"

Come on—the building is not sacred. It is the fellowship of believers that is sacred and pleasing to God. People get mixed up, I guess, thinking the church building somehow pictures the Jewish temple. Personally, I believe we could get a lot more done for Christ by tearing out a few pews, putting up a hoop, and inviting the kids from the neighborhood over for some round ball than we can by catering to some of the stifling saints with their "sacred" lists. Paul wrote:

For Christ didn't send me to baptize, but to preach the Gospel; and even my preaching sounds poor, for I do not fill my sermons with profound words and high sounding ideas, for fear of diluting the mighty power there is in the simple message of the cross of Christ (1 Corinthians 1:17).

I can't count the number of times I have sat in a church pew listening to a preacher talking in terms that would make a seminary graduate scratch his head. Paul said it so plainly. The message of Christ is simple, and powerful, and beautiful. Yet some people continue to contaminate it with arrogant puffiness.

One great hindrance to our being better witnesses, I've noticed, is the feeling that we have to know all the answers to all the questions our non-Christian friends ask. The gospel itself is simple, but many of the questions people raise about it might not be so simple to answer.

I often try to put myself in the shoes of the people outside of Christ and try to see Christians through their eyes, and to be honest, it is scary. One writer put it this way:

We feel supreme love for One we've never seen.
We listen closely to One who never actually speaks.
We entrust our destiny into the hand of One we have
never met.
We empty ourselves in order to be full.
We admit we're wrong so we can be declared right.
We go down in order to get up.

We're strongest when we're weakest.
We're richest when we're poorest.
Our best strategy in battle is on our knees.
Our escape from pressure is standing still.
We die so we can live.
We forsake so we can have.
We surrender so we can conquer.
We see the invisible.
We hear the inaudible.
We believe the incredible.
We understand the inscrutable.
In fact, we know that which passes knowledge.

It isn't hard to see how some people find our message incredible. But we need to keep trying.

The church needs to keep its doors open to everyone. We must allow any kind of person, no matter how sinful, to come into the church and find healing rather than rejection. It doesn't mean we have to accept their present life-style. The hardest group for me to accept personally is rebellious people, those with unteachable spirits, the know-it-alls, those puffed up with knowledge and not open to learning how to live by God's principles.

There are many opportunities to plant and water God's seed in people's hearts—sometimes to those around us at school, at work, in the neighborhood, and sometimes in the church. We have all kinds of people coming through the church doors who are hurting, lonely, defeated. Some of them are coming to the church as a last resort to find a reason for life.

The first place non-Christians look for fulfillment is, of course, in those things that make them feel good, such as drugs, sex, alcohol, and even work. But they find out after a bit that those things really don't satisfy, so after they have tried everything else, it occurs to them that they might just pop their heads into a

church to see if there really is a God and loving people
there. What a responsibility we have to be open and
caring—reaching out to everyone regardless of how
they look, smell, or act!

I think the reason some people look to the church
as the last resort is because of the rejecting, finger-
pointing Christians they have met.

Therefore, when non-Christians come into the
church, we shouldn't expect instant trust. They will be
watching how we live for a while to see if this "God
stuff" is real. It's a tragedy that so many hurting people have to stumble onto the church. We should be
bringing them into the fellowship for emotional and
spiritual healing and repairs. But we have to be crea-
tive—bring them into our homes first so they may
sense our love. Then maybe to a loving Sunday school
class, then maybe to the morning service on Christmas
or Easter or for the kids' play. Little by little, they will
get the point. For sure, don't take them to a member-
ship class for a few years.

Expose your non-Christian friends to your love, plant
some seeds, water them, and God will see to the harvest in his time, making sure they have the strength to
grow. Our responsibility is to love. God's responsibility
is to prepare the person's heart.

As believers, we are all members of the same body,
and each of us has a different job to do in order to
make the body work. We have to be careful not to
look at others and wish we could do what they do or
be like them. I wish I could preach the Word like
Chuck Swindoll, change lives like Bill Gothard, thrill
people with music like Bill and Gloria Gaither, have an
impact on the world like Billy Graham, make the Bible
understandable like Ken Taylor, but I can't because
God has given me a different work to do. None of
these wonderful people will ever live in my neighborhood. They will never work with the same people I

work with, visit our church, and meet my friends. So actually there is no way they could do what God has asked me to do. In effect, I'm just as important in God's eyes to the health of his body, as these talented servants I've mentioned.

Too often we get our eyes on another person's successful ministry and forget the very people to whom God called us to minister. When we are all doing our part, we fit together well and are sensitive to the needs of each of the other parts. Paul wrote:

So, my dear brothers, since future victory is sure, be strong and steady, always abounding in the Lord's work, for you know that nothing you do for the Lord is ever wasted as it would be if there were no resurrection (1 Corinthians 15:58).

This verse is such a comfort to me when I get tired and want to quit. Since the victory is already won through Christ, I can be strong and steady, knowing the outcome of the conflict.

I believe all of our efforts need to be directed in one way or another toward loving people to Christ and this takes time and work. However, some people waste their time arguing among themselves, discussing things that really don't matter in the big picture. We need to concentrate on building a message within ourselves and within the church and then living that message in front of others.

The Holy Spirit lives within us, and that makes us his building—his Church. We are the ones who can change the world by loving other people, because God first loved us.

TWELVE
66 Why Pray? 99

Some years ago I heard a deacon in our church suggest that it really didn't do much good to pray, as God has designed everything to come out a certain way anyway. As I look back on it, he was the kind of teacher who set up straw dummies all the time, and then knocked them down with Scripture.

It could be I missed the knockdown session, because for years I had been inconsistent and powerless in prayer. I lived in fear at church meetings that someone would call on me to pray. I did not have a heart for prayer. I could not use lofty phrases, was pretty much a ham-and-eggs-type prayer, and I assumed my prayers didn't actually bless anyone or get much farther than the ceiling.

Once in a while I would attend a Wednesday night prayer meeting. The men and women would break up into separate groups. I hated to be away from Barb at church because I needed her spiritual support. I was too vulnerable out there on my own, fearing someone might ask me a question I couldn't answer, or want me to quote a verse from the Bible.

As I sat in a circle, praying with the other men, I often wondered how in the world I got there. We would all have to pray in turn, and for some reason I usually wound up being one of the last. By that time everything worthwhile had been prayed for, so I would sit there and strain and think and sweat, trying to come up with something no one else had thought of—the radio ministry, the tract rack, the work party, the library. Just as I would decide on these things to pray for, it would be my luck for the guy sitting next to me to say something like, "And in closing, Lord, we ask your blessing on the radio ministry, the tract rack project, Saturday's work party, and the library. Amen."

Panicsville!

I had heard some of the other men remind God of what had been prayed before, so I would resort to something like, "Dear Lord, as Dave prayed, we hope you'll bless the radio ministry, tract rack, the work party, and the library. And bless everything else everyone has prayed for here tonight. Amen." Needless to say, my Wednesday night prayer meeting attendance was not outstanding.

My primary exposure to prayer was in Sunday school and church. During the evening service, the pastor would call on various people in the congregation to open or close in prayer. I found if I scrunched down in my seat and placed the head of the person sitting in front of me between the pastor and my eyes, most of the time I would escape the assignment of public prayer.

Another thing bothered me—and still does—and that is the practice of being assigned something to pray for, usually something you've never experienced, or someone you have never met, or a situation you have no firsthand knowledge of. My praying, "O Lord, we ask your healing for George's great-aunt's neighbor's boss who has cancer," just doesn't compute with me. A person would bring up a prayer concern, go into great detail on the situation, have a tender heart, a concern, and instead of having that person pray, so often the leader would say, "Chuck, would you pray for that situation?"

Of course I could fake it well, so I got by, but again, I wonder if my prayer ever got past the lightbulbs. How much more logical—how much better it is for the person with the heart for the problem or ministry to bring the matter to God in prayer! They know what they are praying for.

Some churches follow the practice of reciting all the various prayer requests included in the weekly bulletin during the Sunday morning prayer. It sounds like a laundry list, and has about as much meaning for me as the clerk in the Senate reading a bill to the floor. Usually the person praying has no firsthand knowledge about the various people and problems listed in the bulletin, so I suppose they have to peek during the prayer in order to remember everything. I even heard a guy pray one time at a church we attended, "O Lord, you know what Plato said when he...." I would assume the Lord had read all the great works of man and would remember what Plato said. What does all this have to do with making prayer real? I'm sorry, folks. For me, prayer means nothing unless I know the subject firsthand and have a heart's concern for the situation.

It has only been during the last year or so that I have been faithful in regular consistent prayer on my own. I get up fifteen minutes early every morning for prayer. I keep a prayer book where I write down my requests, thanksgiving, and answers. I finally came to the conclusion that since I was God's servant, it was stupid for me to go off half-cocked in the morning without checking with the Master about what he wanted me to do that day. I want to serve him in every way possible, in the way he wants me to serve. I'm not sure if it's my imagination or not, but I'll swear that my days go more smoothly. I get more green lights, more parking spaces, more open bridges than I ever did before I began the program of asking God to direct my path each day.

When I would begin to pray, my mind would wander to some concern at work, or a person, or a situation. And I would feel guilty for getting off the track and force my mind back to the business at hand. Keith Miller suggests a piece of paper handy when we pray to jot down those thoughts that come into mind that are really not related to what is being prayed about. Then I don't worry about forgetting them and can go back to prayer with a new confidence. Sometimes God speaks to us through these "wandering thoughts," especially when we are quiet before him.

I look forward to my time in prayer now, but it has taken many years for me to come to this point. I still have some situations for which I'm not sure if I should bother God or not—for instance, praying for wins in sports.

The big problem is that God has family members on both sides of the line, and my guess is that he has to put his hand over his eyes during the game. That is, except for a recent football season when the University of Washington Huskies played Arizona State in Arizona. There was this psychic in Arizona who predicted that Arizona State would win the game, and not only that, she said they would go on to play in the Rose Bowl. The Huskies had been dodging bullets all season, and Arizona State was blitzing up a storm. So it could be that she might be proven right. In effect, this situation I thought was a "must win" for God, so I prayed for a win. I'm sure I saw a giant finger come down out of the clouds and flick the ball away from Arizona State a couple of times, because there was no way he could allow that psychic to be right.

Washington won the game, but the next week the Huskies' archrivals from across the state knocked them out of a sure trip to the Rose Bowl. Now, all Arizona State had to do was knock off the University of Arizona team, which had not been too spectacular all season, and they would go to the Rose Bowl. So it appeared that maybe the psychic could at least be half right. But Arizona rose to the occasion and won, putting UCLA into the Rose Bowl and the psychic was 100 percent wrong.

I'm still not sure whether I can pray for the Seahawks, Mariners, Huskies, and Sonics to win, but I go through the motions, anyway.

I guess I've heard more legalistic sermons on prayer than I care to remember, all ending up in one great big guilt trip for me. One of my very favorite passages in the Bible talks about prayer:

Don't worry about anything; instead, pray about everything; tell God your needs and don't forget to thank him for his answers. If you do this you will experience God's peace, which is far more wonderful than the human mind can understand. His peace will keep your thoughts and your hearts quiet and at rest as you trust in Christ Jesus (Philippians 4:6, 7).

So many times we quote the first part of this, saying to those around us who are going through struggles and problems, "Don't worry about losing your job; don't worry about your cancer; don't worry about your daughter who is three hours overdue coming home." All we tell people is "don't worry," but they do worry and then feel guilty about it. We supersaints tend to waggle our bony fingers at our friends in legalistic piety, saying in effect, "Obviously you're not too spiritual, since you are worrying." People do worry, and just telling them not to worry won't help. What we need to do is point them to prayer, the solution to worry. Our bodies are simply not designed to handle worry. We need to let God take our problems and handle them for us.

Prayer is not a complicated religious experience. It is simply the natural outflow of a father-child relationship. When we were children we would often cry out to our earthly fathers, asking them to help in some way. Chuck Swindoll once pointed out that as Jesus stepped into the world of Matthew 6, he came into a world filled with religion. The spiritual leaders of that day believed strongly in prayer, but they tied it up with a bunch of man-made rules and traditions that were not based on Scripture. Prayer became formalized, institutionalized, and not spontaneous. They had to pray three times a day, and in a particular position. No matter where they were, or what they were doing, when the time came, they had to stop and do their prayer thing. Where in Scripture did it say to do that? It didn't. The Pharisees said to do it, so the people did it. The prayers also became long and pontifical with all kinds of adjectives before the name of God. "O eternal, matchless, omnipotent, ruler, king, magnificent, marvelous, immortal, etc., etc." I guess the principle was that if they flattered God enough he would give in and do what they wanted.

Can't you just imagine my son wanting to talk with me and starting out: "O marvelous advertising person with a great first serve, photographer, guitar player, etc., etc., etc., Dad. Hear me as I ask you. . . ." That's ridiculous! What he would say is, "Dad, I've got a problem, and here's the situation...." And he would have my ear.

But there is a balance. To stand before the Almighty Creator should fill us with awe and deep respect. To enjoy being in God's presence because we love him as a Father should never cause us to become flippant and disrespectful before him. But God is also our heavenly Father, and he is just as interested (more) as we are in having a close relationship. Jesus said:

Don't recite the same prayer over and over as the heathen do, who think prayers are answered only by repeating them again and again. Remember, your Father knows exactly what you need even before you ask him! (Matthew 6:7, 8).

Another problem with prayers in Jesus' day was that they became repetitious, repeating the same words, often a single word or phrase over and over and over. Where in the Bible does it say to do that? It doesn't, yet this is the practice of some churches, and I don't see how they justify it.

There is often some pride connected with public prayer. When a pastor or other Christian leader comes on a platform before a giant crowd and sits down with his head in his hand to pray, some may think that if he has waited until then to pray, then it's too late. Why didn't he pray in the prayer room where God can hear his requests in secret? Then he can come out onto the platform ready to be a good representative of Jesus Christ—smiling, happy, confident that God will speak through him.

Does that mean I'm against public prayer? Not at all. There are, of course, all kinds of appropriate times for corporate prayer. I pray before and after every class I teach, asking God to open hearts to what he would have us learn from his Word that day. I pray in restaurants when I'm with other Christians—quietly, no big deal—just grateful for the fellowship and the meal he has provided. If I have any doubts whether restaurant or other public prayer would make another person uncomfortable, I pray with my eyes open, and don't try to force them into a painful situation.

I want to win these non-Christian friends—not drive them away. You may not agree, but it's my observation that quite a bit of restaurant and other public prayer is to gain man's attention rather than God's anyway.

How about prayer with our children? Barb and I didn't have our children learn "Now I lay me down to sleep," or the rote prayer at meals. They just observed what we did, and then with a little coaxing, they tried it on their own. I remember they used to pray for the neighbor's dog, the windows, the dishes, Mommy and Daddy, "hope we don't get sick," the neighbor kids, their dolls and toys—everything but the food. At the end we would prompt them, "Remember the food": "Oh yes, and bless this food amen."

I just know God's eyes fill with tears when he listens to children pray. If you really want to know how to pray, listen to children. They can teach you much about being real. Give up all that stuff you've been tossing at God all these years. It's a wonder it doesn't make him sick sometimes.

Another exciting thing to hear is a new Christian praying. A friend of mine came to know Christ recently. The week after he received Christ, we gathered some people at our home—people who had loved him right where he was during his struggle to find God. I remember his first prayer. He started out, "Hi God, this is Jim," and then he went about thanking God for the people sitting in that room who had loved him unconditionally. His prayer was so real, so open, so honest! But it probably would have raised some eyebrows at the Wednesday night prayer meeting, because he didn't use all the "correct" terms, the *thee's* and *thou's.*

Prayer doesn't have to be a bunch of giggles and tinsel either. Some of my most honest prayers have been when I was under terrible burdens of mind. I screamed out, asking God if he really knew what he was doing, allowing me to go through certain situations. I didn't turn into a pile of ashes either. I think he appreciates my honesty. He knows I love him, even though I don't always understand what he is doing in my life. Far too much of my prayer life has been spent doing what was expected rather than what was real. I don't like to feel a distance between God and myself when I pray. I get tired of all the guilt that has been heaped upon me about how, when, where, how long, which words, to pray.

Prayer is not a place, or style, or certain words, or King James English, or position of body. It is a natural outflow of feelings, requests, and thanksgiving from a child to his heavenly Father.

And, by the way, I'm not telling God anything he doesn't already know. He doesn't say, "Mercy me. I didn't know that." For half a century I've been ripped off by folks laying their guilt trips on me about the beautiful world of prayer, and I just thank God for the people and books, and of course, the most important book, the Bible, for helping me begin my pilgrimage of prayer.

Recently I was sitting in my car with the most overwhelming feeling of peace that I have ever experienced in my entire life. And do you know what my next thought was? I wonder when I'm going to get zapped and have something go wrong! And then I think how foolish that is, because God wants my best—he wants me to be joyful and this peace is the logical result of my wanting to serve him with all my heart. He's not some cosmic monster, sitting up on the clouds zapping people who are having fun, or hitting smiling people with lightning. God wants me to have joy in my heart, to have peace, contentment, fulfillment, love. But do you know what the key word is in finding this peace with God? It's called *obedience*. When we obey God and are walking in the center of his will, with our focus in the Word, loving and serving other people, his peace is the natural result. Thank you, Lord, for this beautiful gift. There's a plaque on my mother's wall that says, "Prayer changes things." I agree—and the thing it has changed most is me.

My hope is that before too long, Christ will return and we can fellowship face to face for eternity and I won't need to talk to you by way of a book. What a happy thought! I really don't know how people without Christ face the day. I guess that's why so many of them jump off bridges or take drug overdoses. I probably would have done something like that, too, if God had not, through Christ, reached down his hand to me.

Thanks for traveling with me through this book. Thanks for giving me a little room to be different from you—to have different opinions—and maybe to approach Christianity and its institutions a little differently than you might. But we are members of the same family, parts of the same body, and it takes all of us to make it work.

This has been the story of the pilgrimage of my life so far. I assume that God has many more things for me to learn, more impurities that he has to burn out of my life, more struggles for me to endure so that I can be more valuable to others by sharing the comfort God gives me through each situation.

Christ is real to me, and no one can do or say anything that would make him any less real. I've proved his reality to my satisfaction, and that's something no one can argue with.

I love the story about the blind man Christ healed. Afterward some of the religious men of the day were talking to the former blind man saying some awful things about Christ. The man said something that brings tears to my eyes every time I read it. Imagine him standing there with those pious leaders saying, "All I know is that once I was blind, but now I can see."

And other than that, I have no opinion.

God bless you,

CHUCK SNYDER